D1248324

UP FROM
the Minor Leagues of
HOCKEY

UP FROM
the Minor Leagues of
HOCKEY

Stan & Shirley Fischler

COWLES BOOK COMPANY, INC.
A subsidiary of Henry Regnery Co.

Copyright © 1971 by Stan and Shirley Fischler. All rights reserved.
Published by Cowles Book Company, Inc.
A subsidiary of Henry Regnery Company
114 West Illinois Street, Chicago, Illinois 60610
Manufactured in the United States of America
Library of Congress Catalog Card Number: 71—163280

Contents

Preface

Once upon a time — frankly, we don't remember when — a philosopher observed that pain and progress are inseparable. Nowhere is this maxim more relevant than in the saga of minor league hockey players as they ply the often long and torturous route to the National Hockey League — the majors.

Some players, who deserved a better fate, never made it. That happened mostly before the NHL expanded from 6 to 12 teams in 1967 and, again, to 14 teams in 1970. Others, such as Aldo Guidolin of the Rangers, enjoyed only a brief fling before being unjustly demoted. And still others, including Larry Zeidel of the Philadelphia Flyers, received their recognition far too late in their hockey life to make the most of it. Zeidel was 39 years old when the Flyers hired him.

But even the rejects, the people who never climbed past the American or Western or International or Eastern Leagues, never really resented their hockey experiences because, to a man, they were being paid to play a game they enjoyed more than any other, and money really can't buy that kind of pleasure.

Make no mistake: the joys of playing hockey can be diminished by other circumstances; and that explains why the trek up from the minors is so difficult. To Ernie Wakely, the St. Louis Blues goalie, it was the constant shuttling from one city to another, leaving his wife behind until he could settle in a new base, only to find he was being shunted to still another town. Within two years Wakely played in Hull-Ottawa, Kingston, North Bay (all in Ontario), Montreal, Quebec, and Spokane, Washington.

"The traveling," said Wakely, "was the worst thing. It would get awfully tiresome."

To others, such as Doug Barkley, the Detroit Red Wings coach, and Ed Van Impe, the Philadelphia Flyers defenseman, the long wait in the minors grated because they thought they belonged on top. They watched from the Western and American Leagues as their parent clubs elevated players who were obviously inferior to them, and they wondered whether they would ever be discovered.

For them, the perennial motto, "Genius will out," didn't seem to hold any water. But just when all appeared lost, they *were,* in fact, sighted and brought to the big time.

Some players, such as Jean Ratelle of the New York Rangers, were imported too soon with too great a build-up to a team desperate for success. Failure inevitably resulted, and Ratelle was dispatched to Baltimore. There, ironically, it was Aldo Guidolin, now the Baltimore coach, a man who never got the big chance in the NHL, who restored Ratelle's confidence, enabling him eventually to attain NHL stardom.

Then there is the case of John Ferguson, a man with the most limited abilities in skating, shooting, and passing, who honed his assets to sharpness through grueling practices in places such as Melville, Saskatchewan, Fort Wayne, Indiana, and Cleveland, Ohio, before reaching his big-league goal with the Montreal Canadiens. Never has there been a better demonstration of how perseverance and grim determination can pay dividends in hockey than in Ferguson's example.

In some cases the handicaps were greater than others. Barkley had to overcome two damaging injuries to his knees; Binkley was near-sighted and played goal, the most dangerous position, wearing contact lenses; Dennis Hull had to cope with the burden of the famous Hull name, glamorized by his brother Bobby.

Reggie Fleming came up from the boondocks as a "policeman," the hockey tough guy who protects his smaller teammates. To make it in the NHL he first had to fight his way through the minors. A couple of bad beatings here and there would have made him a goner.

For the most part, hockey's Law of Averages hung true in the realm of coaching. There were good ones, and there were always the few bad ones; and then there was Eddie Shore at Springfield, who influenced nearly every minor leaguer in one way or another whether they played with Shore's club or against it. The chapter about Shore speaks for itself.

In writing the book we decided early to let the players themselves tell their own story with a minimum of commentary by the authors. As Lawrence Ritter, author of the baseball classic *The Glory of Their Times,* once pointed out, most history is written long after the event by outsiders trying to reconstruct the events, and too often the reconstruction is faulty. Here we have the minor league experiences related directly by those who did the experiencing.

Perhaps the most enjoyable part of putting together this book was the act of gathering material. For starters, we decided to select a representative group of NHL players — representative in *every* way.

We have one coach, two goaltenders, one defenseman, two

forwards, and one utility player. In Jean Ratelle, we have a high-scoring gentlemanly player; in Reg Fleming, a low-scoring tough guy. Dennis Hull reached the NHL when he was relatively young (20), and Les Binkley didn't make it until he was 33. At this writing, four of the subjects are in the East Division and four in the West.

To make contact with some of the players we needed help from their team publicists. Paul Wieland of Buffalo, Terry Schiffhauer of Pittsburgh, Joe Varga of Detroit, Gary Ronberg of St. Louis, and Joe Kadlec of Philadelphia proved invaluable in their assistance.

Those players included here were, to a man, gracious, courteous, and helpful. Some, such as Binkley and Ferguson, were friends from past stories; others, such as Van Impe and Barkley, were being interviewed by us for the first time.

In many cases the interviews were conducted under an atmosphere of pressure. On the day of our interview, Binkley, Ferguson, and Fleming were preparing for a game that night against the Rangers in Madison Square Garden. During his interview, Barkley, who had just taken over as coach of the Red Wings, was worried about his game against Philadelphia that night at the Spectrum.

By contrast, the interviews with Van Impe and Ratelle were relaxed; they took place in their respective living rooms on an afternoon following a game.

In most cases the players talked about things unrelated to their minor league experiences as well as discussing the subject of this book. They reminisced about their home towns — Ratelle comes from French Canada and the others, from various parts of English-speaking Canada — and their childhood days when they were skating as much on their ankles as they were on their blades.

To obtain the material we used a tape recorder in each instance, but at no time did the machine seem to interfere with the player's candor. After transcribing the tapes to typewritten pages, we did a certain amount of editing to obtain a reasonable chronological sequence.

The editing, however, has been minor, and the words on these pages are predominantly the words of the individual players. Curiously, the players did sometimes forget names of teams and dates from their dim, distant past. This, however, was the exception rather than the rule.

What follows are the stories of what it was like from the day each of these accomplished professionals laced on their first pair of skates to the day they reached their Holy Grail — the National Hockey League.

This is the way it is on the way up from the minor leagues of hockey!

STAN AND SHIRLEY FISCHLER

Hockey's Curious
Minor League System

WHILE gathering material for this book, the authors realized that nowhere in the literature of hockey is there a simple explanation of either the amateur or the professional minor league system and its structure.

As the players, whose experiences are about to be revealed on the following pages, related their travels through this system, a confusing picture began to develop: the picture of a system that seemed somewhat like the Little Leagues of an American sport — with Pee Wee, Bantam, and Midget categories for young people — but that also seemed to make "property" out of 12-year-old children.

The fact that a boy of that age almost invariably became the property of a National League franchise is a distinctly "un-American" and non-amateur approach to a sport. Yet this is the system as it existed in Canada until 1967: Reggie Fleming became the property of the Montreal Canadiens when he entered Midget hockey at age 13; Jean Ratelle belonged to the New York Rangers at age 16, when he signed with Ranger scout Yvon Prud'Homme.

But here is the paradox: the system as it is described by each player in this book no longer exists because of the introduction of a new relationship between the Canadian Amateur Hockey Association (CAHA) and the National Hockey League (NHL) in 1967, prior to the expansion of the NHL from six to twelve teams.

Therefore, we decided that a rudimentary explanation of the system would be essential to a book dealing with hockey's minor leagues. This proved to be much more difficult than we originally supposed, since the entire system apparently cannot be explained or described by any one source or any one expert on hockey. Therefore, we give many thanks to Leo Ornest, NHL Director of Publications; Eugene Kinasewich, former president of the Western Hockey League; and Thomas F. Lockhart, President of the Amateur Hockey Association of the United States, for their contributions to the explanation of the amateur and minor professional hockey structure as it exists today.

Amateur hockey is entirely under the jurisdiction of the CAHA and the American Hockey Association (AHA) in the United States. Under the wing of the CAHA are the Canadian provincial hockey associations, such as the Ontario Hockey Association, and the district hockey associations, such as the Metropolitan Hockey Associations of Toronto and Montreal. Within these provincial and district associations hockey is broken down by age group levels, somewhat similar to Little Leagues in American baseball.

Pee Wee hockey is the lowest, or youngest, category, including all boys under the age of 12. Within the category of Pee Wee, depending on the size of the league and the number of boys in an age group, Pee Wee may be subdivided into such categories as "Atom," "Squirt," "Tyke," or other categories, for boys age six to eight, eight to ten, and ten to twelve. The next level is Bantam hockey, for boys under the age of 14; then Midget for boys under 16; Juvenile for under 18; and finally Junior hockey.

At this point the system gets confusing again, for after Juvenile hockey, there are actually three avenues that an aspiring player can enter. If he chooses to go to college, he will probably go to the United States because college hockey in Canada is, at this time, poorly developed — due in part to the immense geographical distance between the few Canadian colleges and in part to poor financial support for the players. This will be changing in Canada soon, for a great deal of pressure is being exerted on colleges to offer hockey scholarships, and the NHL and CAHA are receiving pressure to begin subsidizing college hockey.

The second choice for a player after Juvenile is Intermediate hockey, which is a very small, weak league in Canada, offering straight amateur status to the player without the pressures of Junior hockey. From there the player can go up to the Senior Leagues of Canada, the highest level of amateur status in the country.

The third path, the one taken by nearly all potential professionals, is the move to Junior hockey, which includes players from age 16 through 21. At the end of his Junior career, a player is eligible to be drafted into the professional leagues. And within the Junior system there are also two categories: Junior A and Junior B, a simple division according to ability.

Before 1967 a player 18 years of age could be signed by a National Hockey League club (if he had not been signed earlier) by virtue of the now extinct "A," "B," or "C" form. The player was then the indisputable property of that NHL franchise and could be moved up into the minor pros or even the NHL, as his parent organization saw fit.

Each of the players in this book signed such a form, and each spent his Junior career as the property of an NHL franchise.

With the advent of expansion, however, the necessity for releasing talent to the new, needy clubs, the NHL and the CAHA (and the AHA in the United States) signed an agreement whereby all amateur hockey, including Junior hockey, became solely the domain of the CAHA. It was no longer possible for an NHL club to own a Junior club simply because they were interested in owning *one* talented player, as the Boston Bruins owned the Oshawa Junior A team purely because they wanted the gigantic abilities of Bobby Orr.

Today the NHL sponsors amateur and Junior hockey only through the payment of Annual Assessments and Player Development Funds to the CAHA. And for every player the NHL drafts out of the Junior system and into the pros, the NHL must repay the CAHA with a Draft Claim Payment. The Universal Draft System is structured so that the weakest NHL club of any given season has the first draft choice from the Junior talent (although there has been a great deal of trading draft choices among the NHL teams, and consequently some of the old, established teams have some of the best draft choices).

In the actual minor pro system there are the Western, Central, and American Hockey Leagues, which are totally professional. The International and Eastern Hockey Leagues are officially "amateur" leagues under the jurisdiction of the CAHA, equal to the Canadian Senior Hockey leagues and consisting mainly of drafted amateurs, reinstated amateurs, or retired professionals who have been waived out of professional hockey. Ironically, many of these "amateurs" earn as much as professional players, but the definition of a professional in hockey is quite simply someone who has signed a standard player's contract with a professional team.

The Western and American Leagues are theoretically autonomous from the NHL, but because further expansion of the NHL in 1970 has necessitated enlargement of the farm system, certain clubs in the American Hockey League are now affiliated with NHL franchises. And in the Western Hockey League, teams also are affiliated with NHL franchises.

If a minor professional club is affiliated with an NHL franchise, there are definite rules that determine the composition of the team. The Central Hockey League is officially the league that contains the "development," or farm, clubs for the NHL. Under the development club rules there must be a certain number of players on each team who are under the age of 23 and a certain number under the age of 26. This means, of course, that most of the older veterans and former NHL pros who have been "sent down" are now playing in the American or Western Leagues.

This, then, is the basic structure of minor professional hockey. And although the system has changed radically from the days described by the characters in this book, the quality, indeed the survival, of the sport depends, as it always has, on the ability of the minor leagues to develop talent for the National Hockey League.

"To me, the $64 question isn't whether you can hand it out but whether you can *take* it."

— *Eddie Shore*

1

Eddie Shore's Springfield

N O SPORTS franchise, be it in baseball, football, basketball, or hockey, so epitomizes what we have come to understand as "minor league" than the Springfield (Massachusetts) Indians of the American Hockey League, circa 1947-1967.

Only one factor was necessary to set Springfield apart from the others, but that factor was crucial because it involved the most amazing — and easily the most bizarre — personality ever to run a professional athletic team.

His name is Eddie Shore.

Shore was born on a farm in Fort Qu'Appelle-Cupar, Saskatchewan, and he toughened himself early in life, hauling the harvested grain to town and riding wild horses. In time he was to become one of the most accomplished and feared defensemen ever to skate in the National Hockey League.

Shore arrived in the big time in 1926 and singlehandedly built the Boston Bruins into an NHL power. His end-to-end puck-carrying rushes soon became legendary, matched in excitement only by his crunching bodychecks and his ability to sustain great pain.

While earning a place on the All-Star team eight times and being named the NHL's most valuable player four times, Shore accumulated more than 900 stitches in his body, not to mention fractures of his back, hip, and collarbone. His nose was broken 14 times and his jaw smashed 5 times.

Shore retired from full-time play in 1940 and invested his savings in the acquisition of the Springfield hockey club. His investment was a major one and, no doubt, helped to shape Shore's budgetary philosophy, which, according to some observers, was somewhat to the right of frugality.

"When he first got the franchise," said Jack Riley, former president of the American League, "he used to park cars outside the arena until about ten minutes before game time. Then Eddie would go in, suit up, and play defense for his team.

"His players would take inner tubes from their automobile tires, cut them up into rubber bands and put them around hockey stockings to save the cost of tape. During the ice show at the arena, Eddie operated one of the spotlights himself to save expenses. But you can't knock him. Not when he invested all his hockey money right back where it came from."

Shore paid $42,000 for the Indians — $16,000 in cash and the rest on a note — and he was determined to build Springfield into one of the best hockey cities on the continent. In a sense, he succeeded. Attendance at home games reached a profitable level in time, and Shore developed an excellent hockey program for the young people in the city.

But Eddie was never content to limit himself to the front office part of the business. Over the years he had developed innumerable theories about the way hockey should be played, and he was determined to pass these ideas along to his players. More than anything it was Shore the theoretician, the coach, and the manager that marked him as the only one of his kind in the world. His actions also explain why many skaters considered Springfield the Siberia of minor league hockey.

How can anyone believe a man would open a training camp by ordering two dozen rugged hockey players to tap dance in the hotel lobby or to execute delicate ballet steps on ice? Would an ordinary coach tape a player's hands to his stick? Or work out day after day with his players despite four near-fatal heart attacks? Is it conceivable that a club owner would instruct players' wives to diminish sexual relations with their husbands in the interests of a winning team? Is it imaginable, either, that a man would actually lock a referee out of his dressing room as punishment for "poor" officiating? Or order his players to make popcorn, blow up balloons, and sell programs when they're not in the game?

"You better believe it happens with Shore," said Don Johns, an alumnus of Shore's Indians. "Once Eddie told me he knew why I wasn't a better hockey player. I'm always willing to learn. So I said, 'Okay, Ed, what's wrong with me?' Know what he says? 'You're not *combing your hair* right.' He told me to part it on the other side. That way it would help me 'cause I'd have something to think about."

Johns was struck dumb at the opening of training camp. Several players were churning up and down the ice taking shots on goal when a whistle pierced the air. Shore beckoned to a rookie, and the other players stopped to see what Eddie was up to this time. "He wanted the boy to skate with his legs closer," said Johns, "so he pulled out a piece of cord and tied the kid's legs together and told him to skate. Did you ever try to skate with your legs tied?"

Another time, Johns was immobilized on a hospital bed after suffering a 40-stitch cut in his leg. The phone rang. It was Shore. " 'Mis-ter Johns,' he said, 'you ought to be ready to play soon.' "

" 'But, Eddie,' I told him, 'I can't even turn my leg . . . ' Next thing I knew he hung up. For a minute I thought maybe I was babying myself. So I called the doc and told him to look at the leg. He did, and he told me I'd be crazy if I got outa bed in the next couple of days."

By the end of the week, Johns was released from the hospital, and he reported to Shore, who occupied a modest office in the Eastern States Coliseum, the rink he leases in West Springfield, Massachusetts.

"Mis-ter Johns," Shore ordered, "you're playing tonight."

"He played me for three minutes," said Johns, "and then suspended me for a week.

" 'When I played hockey,' Shore told me, 'I once had a hundred stitches in my leg, and I was out only three — no, two and a half — days.' "

After a few weeks, Johns had become numbed by Shore's criticism. Johns's feet were wrong. Shore said: he wasn't shooting correctly or bending properly, and so on, *ad nauseam.*

One day, when Johns was about to quit, Shore pointed at him. "Mis-ter Johns," he said, "What did you do wrong *this* time?"

Exasperated, Johns said, "I guess I wasn't skating right. Or my hands were too close on the stick . . ."

"Bul-loney," Shore said. "You're doing *nothing* wrong."

Johns considers himself rather fortunate that he was sent to Baltimore after only a year in Springfield. Others, such as Billy McCreary, formerly of the St. Louis Blues, who played four years for Shore, curse the day they were told to report. Up to his ears in Shore-isms, McCreary once threatened to quit hockey rather than to sign another Springfield contract. Eddie finally traded him to Hull-Ottawa.

McCreary says Shore was so cheap he made Jack Benny

seem like the last of the great spenders. "We were on strict budgets with him," said McCreary. "He allowed us to tip taxi drivers fifteen cents. After a while, we got so known around the league, none of the cabbies wanted to pick us up.

"That was bad enough. But some guys had a bonus clause in their contracts. If they got, say, thirty goals, they'd get more money. So a guy would be comin' close to thirty near the end of the season. Does he make it? Hell, Shore would sit him out of the last five games so he couldn't score any more. And if you think I'm joking, just ask any player who skated for Shore."

Still, when polling members of the Shore Alumni Association, a fellow can find as many admirers of the "Old Man" as critics. Everybody agrees, though, that Shore is the wildest, most learned hockey man in the world.

One graduate of Shoresville, Don Simmons, former goaltender for the Stanley Cup champion Toronto Maple Leafs, says Shore's techniques left him limp from shock. "I'll never forget how Eddie hated to see his goalkeepers fall to the ice. If he got a player and that poor sap fell down to block a shot — like Nipper O'Hearn or Johnny Henderson used to — Shore'd get a piece of twine and tie the goalie's arm to the crossbar of the net. Then he'd dare him to fall."

Shore once ordered Simmons into his office. Don had been in a slump and, naturally, feared the worst. But Eddie was convinced Simmons had developed a mental block against goaltending. He suggested that the kid return to his home in Port Colborne, Ontario, for a rest. "He told me to go home to my mother. 'Help her around the house,' he said. 'Wash the dishes and do other chores for her. That'll take your mind off hockey. While you're at it, find a studio and take some dancing lessons.' "

Simmons nearly suffered a nervous breakdown soon after he returned. In a tense game between Cleveland and Springfield, referee Frank Udvari called a penalty against the

Indians that so enraged Shore he ordered his entire team off the ice with the exception of Simmons. Udvari pulled out his watch. "You got ten seconds to ice a team," the referee said, "or I drop the puck." Shore ignored the threat.·

Udvari dropped the puck, and five Cleveland players charged at Simmons. So amazed were the attackers at this unheard-of scoring opportunity, they fought among themselves over who would take the shot. Finally, Bo Elik of Cleveland shot and missed. Three succeeding shots went wild, and Simmons fell on the puck, stopping play. Finally, Shore sent his team back on the ice.

The players' wives became involved in the bizarre world of Eddie Shore one day several years ago during a losing streak. A notice was posted on the team bulletin board: "Players and Wives Report to Dressing Room at 3 P.M."

"We thought it would be a party," said Simmons, "because the Old Man threw a party every once in a while. We told our wives to get dressed up real fine. When we got to the dressing room the girls expected to see decorations. Instead, the room was filled with dirty uniforms and stunk of liniment. That shook them up a bit, but nothing like what was to come.

"After we all sat down, the Old Man looked at our wives and said the team wasn't doing as well as it should. He told the girls he wanted them to pay less attention to their husbands so we could play better hockey for the rest of the season. Then he sent us home. That was the end of the party."

Although Shore had four heart attacks, he would throw himself into furies, even fighting opposing players. Such combat was relatively simple for Eddie since the Coliseum's penalty box was directly across the aisle from the Springfield bench. All Shore had to do was leave his seat behind the bench and walk a few feet to the penalty box.

On one such walk, Shore nearly gave his doctor a heart attack. Aldo Guidolin, the tough former Cleveland defenseman, was penalized after manhandling several Springfield players. As Guidolin stepped into the penalty box, Shore charged him. "He told me," said Guidolin, "if he was 20 years younger, he'd kick the crap outa me. That didn't satisfy him 'cause we beat 'em in overtime. So, after the game, he ran down to the announcer's box, turned on the loudspeaker, and called the referee every name in the book. You could hear it all over the rink."

Another alumnus of Shore Academy, class of 1959, Guidolin shudders when he recalls the hours of grim instruction with Eddie. "He harped on three points," said Guidolin. "He wants the hands two feet apart on the stick, the feet eleven inches apart on the ice, and he wants you to skate in a sort of sitting position. You better do it exactly right, or you're in big trouble."

Guidolin discovered this one morning during a practice. He had just completed what he considered a perfect pass that resulted in a goal. What's more he had skated at top speed while doing it. Then he heard the whistle and saw Shore motion to him. "Mis-ter Guidolin," he said, "do you know what you did wrong?"

"The pass was perfect," said Guidolin. "I was in the sitting position. My two hands were on the stick. What more do you want?"

"Mis-ter Guidolin," Shore said, "your legs were *two inches* too far apart."

As outlandish as Shore's ideas may first appear, they are well grounded in physiological theory developed and harbored in his encyclopedic mind. "Studying under Shore is like getting your doctorate in hockey science," said Kent Douglas, once Toronto's star defenseman. "The Old Man taught me things about the game nobody else ever mentioned. He showed me you don't have to hit a man real hard — just get a piece of him. He showed me how you maneuver a man till he's off balance. Then you take the puck away from him."

When Douglas complained about being overweight, Shore stayed up nights analyzing the problem. Finally, he had the solution. "You're drinking too much water," Eddie said. Douglas eliminated excess water from his diet, lost weight, gained speed and stamina, and won the American League's outstanding defenseman's trophy.

Shore startled Guidolin and a dozen other players when he ordered them to try several dance routines. But Eddie could see nothing to be surprised about. Not when his lesson made all the sense in the world.

"Tap dancing," Shore explained, "improves balance, and balance is the foundation of an athlete's ability. From balance he obtains power and maneuverability. I want a player to move forward, backward, to one side or the other without actually taking a step, just by shifting his balance. Add those up each time he has to make a move during a game, and he's saving himself a tremendous amount of energy."

Another Shore theory was that players should skate from an almost sitting position. "You fellows were in the Boy Scouts," he'd say. "Remember when you were on a hike in the woods and had to move your bowels? You'd have to bend your knees and squat. Well, that's the way I want you to skate."

Eddie felt that the hockey stick is as delicate a tool as a gyroscope. He urged his players to use nothing but a six- to eight-lie (the angle between the blade and the shaft) stick. This often disturbed players who had been used to four- or nine-lie sticks. Springfield's former star scorer, Bill Sweeney, always preferred a four-lie but rather than quarrel with Shore, he told him that he would use six-lie sticks.

"Sweeney fooled the Old Man," said Guidolin. "He had his four-lie stick stamped six, and Shore never knew the difference."

Eddie's severest critics were members of the "Black Aces,"

Indians out of the lineup as a result of injury, illness, or Shore's desire to bench them. However, they often were compelled to work considerably harder than regular members of the team. "Shore used to tell the Black Aces he's paying like any other job where you put in an eight-hour day," said Hershey defenseman Larry Zeidel. "So he'd have 'em at the rink all day and told 'em to bring a lunch bucket."

The Black Aces said they were forced to do such odd jobs as paint arena seats, sell programs, make popcorn, and blow up hundreds of balloons before ice shows. Once, when some Aces were particularly angry, they gave Shore a special lesson in balance. It happened when Eddie was changing a light bulb in the Coliseum's high ceiling — he *never* required anyone to perform a job he wouldn't do. To do this, he had to climb a platform which the players on ice pushed from bulb to bulb. At one point Shore was hanging onto an overhead cable with one hand. screwing in a bulb with another, when someone "accidentally" pushed the tower from under him. "He was just hanging there from the cables like a trapeze artist," said a former Ace. "The fellas finally got around to pushing the platform back so he could get down."

According to several men, Shore treated his coaches the same way he treated his Black Aces. Pat Egan, the erstwhile Springfield coach, reportedly painted the arena seats, scraped the ice, and repaired Shore's house.

Opposing coaches suffered too, when they were in Springfield. When King Clancy was coaching Cincinnati, Shore said he'd allow Clancy use of the Coliseum ice for morning practice. The Coliseum is a barnlike structure with a seating capacity of 5,600 and rows of windows near the ceiling on either side of the ice. Late in the morning, the sun beams through the windows giving the rink its only natural light and warmth. But this, of course, is contingent on the sun coming out.

"We got on the ice at nine in the morning," said New York

Rangers manager Emile Francis, then playing for Cincinnati. "The place was dark as the Dickens, so I asked Clancy to get the lights put on. Just then, Shore came by.

" 'Hey, Eddie,' Clancy yells, 'how about giving us some light for the practice?' "

"Ya know what Shore tells him. He said, 'Wait a half hour till the sun rises and comes through the windows Then you'll have plenty of light.' "

At the game the next night, Clancy climbed over the boards, marched solemnly across the ice, and presented Shore with a lantern.

Shore has managed to antagonize almost every coach in the league, but none more than Jackie Gordon. In a February, 1960, game with Cleveland, Shore suffered a fit of pique when referee Lou Farelli disallowed a Springfield goal even though goal judge Bill Tebone had flashed the red light signifying the point.

Gordon, then the Cleveland coach, couldn't believe it when Eddie reacted by removing Tebone from his post behind the net. Shore said that if the referee could overrule the goal judge, there was no point having one. Gordon insisted the least Shore could do was appoint a new judge. Farelli ordered Shore to comply, but Eddie wouldn't hear of it. The referee resumed the game — minus one very important official.

"I did *not* pull out the goal judge," Shore said. "He saw the puck go in and put the light on. The referee would not take his decision. So the judge said: 'I seen the puck in. I'm not a liar. If I am, I don't want the job.' So he walked away.

"The referee asked me to put in another judge. I said, 'This man is honest. If I put in another man it would be saying the first man is a liar and a cheat,' I told the referee: 'Either he goes back in there or else you don't have a goal judge.' "

Ultimately, the then league president Richard Canning fined Shore $2,000 for the stunt. Eddie suffered a heart attack thereafter. "When he had the attack," said the late Jim Ellery, secretary-treasurer of the American League, "we decided not to press him for the money. And never have."

Fining without collecting is a formula followed by Shore himself. This is the other side of Shore, the side as hidden from the public as the far side of the moon. He's steel on the outside but soft as cotton candy underneath. But he never talks about it. You have to talk to Shore's friends to learn that he donated thousands of dollars to cover hospital expenses when forward Doug McMurdy's son was seriously injured. Eddie will not tell you that he gave Bill Sweeney $1,000 to pull him out of a financial jam or that he performed countless other acts of benevolence.

One night Shore caught a couple of players drinking after hours and fined each $200. At the end of the season each received a $200 bonus. Another time, Eddie criticized Ken Schinkel for a mistake during a workout. Normally mild-mannered, Schinkel was upset because his wife had just lost a baby. "Eddie," Schinkel shouted, "you can go to hell."

"That'll cost you $100," snapped Shore.

After the playoffs, Schinkel dropped into the hockey office to say goodbye to his boss. "Wait a minute," said Shore, reaching into his pocket and pulling out $100. "I don't know why I'm so good to you."

"Funny thing about him," said Schinkel. "He fined me every year I was ever there, but every year he gave me the money back. One thing you gotta say for Eddie — he stuck up for his players all the way."

Eddie's bizarre behavior reached in many directions, including the world of medicine. He's always fancied himself an amateur doctor, trainer, and psychologist, and he insists he cured himself twice of cancer, once of the bowels and once of the liver. "He went on a special starvation diet," said Larry Zeidel, "and he says he eventually passed it out of his system."

Eddie himself didn't care to discuss the bouts with cancer. "All I can say," he said, "is three specialists gave me only six months to live in 1940."

Shore passed his medicinal advice to his players. One afternoon he noticed Schinkel sniffling. Ken had a cold and, having tried the usual remedies without success, was simply waiting out the ailment. Shore had other ideas. "You know what he prescribed?" said Schinkel. "Twelve drops of iodine. And you know what? It worked!"

Sometimes the Shore cure — or diagnosis — disagrees with the patient. Eddie once told Schinkel he was suffering from yellow jaundice. "The Old Man gave me his special 'Marlet Treatment,'" said Schinkel. "It was a laxative made up of oils. I was scared of it, so I only took half of what I was supposed to. I lost twelve pounds in no time, so I cut it out. I think if I'd taken the whole business it would've been suicide."

The surest form of suicide in Springfield was a full-scale attempt to buck Shore's will. Occasionally, he'd put up with a player who disputed him if he believed the player had a point. But it wasn't any healthier to quarrel with Eddie off ice than it was on.

Former Springfield broadcaster Bob Jones once accused Shore of having him fined for discussing player gripes on the radio. "When I took up the cudgel and aired some of the grievances of my friends on the team I was removed from the air," said Jones. "I thought Shore's penchant for having players sweep the ice, pick up debris, and sell score cards was anything but funny.

"What has made the whole era of Shore-dominated sport so mystifying to the average Springfield fan was this: *they didn't know anything about it.* The two local papers never printed a derogatory word about him. The miserable morale of the Springfield club, which led to a succession of losing seasons, was glossed over or completely ignored."

Perhaps it was, but in the 1966-1967 season the Springfield hockey players rose in revolt against their master, in what developed into one of the ice game's rare full-scale mutinies. The players laid it on the line with Shore -- either he shaped up, or they would ship out. This was not the first time that Shore had been challenged, but it was one of the rare times when he was defeated.

The pivotal factor was timing. It had become the age of revolt throughout the world, and NHL players had turned to Toronto attorney R. Alan Eagleson for help in organizing a Players' Association. When the Springfield players heard about Eagleson, they contacted him, and he immediately became the general of their uprising.

"I got tired of Shore talking to me like an animal," said Roger Cote, a defenseman who had challenged Shore's practices. "I haven't been paid for weeks. But Mr. Eagleson says not to worry."

The players remained firm in their stand, and public opinion in the hockey world soon turned against Shore. He eventually yielded to the pressure. Shore turned the team over to his son Eddie, Jr., and eventually he delivered control of it to the Los Angeles Kings when Los Angeles joined the NHL in the first major expansion.

Shore himself always believed he was doing the right thing — for hockey, for his players, and for himself. In an interview during his heyday as owner of the Indians, he discussed his image and his impact with the authors.

"To me," Shore said, "the $64 question isn't whether you can hand it out but whether you can *take* it . . . ."

Asked about his image and its not so positive side, he said: "I'll tell you what's the matter. Shore has always been in the wrong. He doesn't mean to be, but he gets in people's bad graces. He's been outspoken even if it hurts. But his shoulders are fairly broad. I see no point in bragging. I've always felt the truth will out."

Each year the NHL presents the Lester Patrick Trophy. It is given to the man who has done outstanding work for hockey in the United States. Gordie Howe has won it. Bobby Hull has won it.

In March 1970 the winner was Eddie Shore.

"Most of us are a little crazy in some form or other," Shore once said. "Some of us admit it. As for me, I'm not sorry about *anything* I've ever done in my life. As long as I can be close to hockey, I'm happy to be alive!"

"It wasn't as simple as just jumping out of a trainer's white suit and becoming a professional goaltender."

— *Les Binkley*

2

Les Binkley

When newspapermen talked about Les Binkley, they made it sound all so easy, so sensational.

One day in 1958 he was the trainer for the Cleveland Barons in the American League; the next day he was the Barons' star goalkeeper. "From Training Table to Goal Crease" shouted the headlines.

The fact is, however, that such miracles don't really happen in pro hockey. In order to make the grade as a professional goaltender, the 6', 175-pound Binkley toiled many long, hard years in the minors. He accepted the job as trainer only because it allowed him to work out as the Barons' practice goalie.

When, after a long career in the bushes, Les finally reached the National Hockey League, he was hailed as a superior goaltender. "There are several goalies who get more publicity," said Boston Bruins scout Red Sullivan, "but outside of maybe one other goaltender, there is no one who has more ability than Binkley."

In the 1967-1968 campaign, Binkley's first season in the NHL, he was given a standing ovation in Boston Garden after shutting out the high-scoring Bruins. One night he robbed Brit Selby of a sure goal at the Spectrum in Philadelphia, spearing the puck with a split-second glove save. "In all my life," said Philadelphia defenseman Joe Watson, "I've never seen a save like that."

Others have said that they've never seen a goalie like Binkley before. He wears contact lenses on the ice and regular glasses when he is not playing. He resembles an accountant more than a man who performs the most difficult job in sports.

"Binkley looks somewhat like he sounds," wrote Hugh Brown of the Philadelphia Bulletin. *"meaning he could pass for a nearsighted, narrow-chested birdwatcher."*

Our interview with Les took place in November 1970 in the dining room of the Park Sheraton Hotel opposite Madison Square Garden. Scheduled to face the Rangers that night, the Penguins were having their pregame meal when Les and the authors discussed his minor league experiences. He wore a conservatively tailored gray suit and looked like anything but an NHL goalie.

He takes his job seriously but with a sprinkling of salt here and there. Les admitted that he had decided to use the protective face mask during the 1970-1971 season because opponents were shooting the puck harder than ever. He laughed. "If I had my way, I'd change the rules and have them substitute a tennis ball for the hard rubber puck!"

I GREW up in Owen Sound, Ontario, a small city of about 20,000 people on big Georgian Bay in northern Ontario. It was a good place to learn hockey because the winters were severe, and there was always ice around to learn to skate on. Another advantage for me was the fact that my father, who was a railroad man, had once been a semi-pro baseball player. He always enjoyed competitive sports, and he encouraged me to play.

When I was about five years old, I got my first pair of ice skates. There was plenty of opportunity to use them since we had five outdoor rinks for skating and a big indoor rink. Most of the time, at the start, I skated on the outdoor rinks. I'll tell you, it got awfully chilly out there — sometimes 'way below zero — and you had a good chance to freeze your toes if you didn't move around quite a bit. But in my neighborhood everyone seemed willing to play or practice or just do ordinary skating.

Early in my skating career I began playing a wing position. I was about 11 years old, and I enjoyed skating, but lots of times we'd do variations on hockey because we loved it so much. For example, one of the variations was a game called "road hockey," which could be played going to and from school and could be played also in the warmer months. Instead of using skates, you run around in your regular shoes and play on the streets instead of a rink.

In street hockey we'd use a tin can, a tennis ball, or something like that instead of a regular rubber hockey puck. Sometimes in the winter, we wouldn't even bother going to the rink. After dinner, a bunch of us would place two snowballs at one end of the street and two snowballs at the other end — marking off the "goalposts" — and play hockey under a street light until we were exhausted. The interesting thing is that those street hockey games when I was a kid turned out to be the turning point in my career. I had been playing forward in regular ice hockey games, but in street hockey I used to just stand there in goal and, somehow, I became a pretty good goaltender in those games.

One day when we were playing ice hockey, our regular goaltender got hurt, and the guys remembered that I had played goal in street hockey. "Why don't you play goal for us, Les?" one of my friends asked me. "You always play goal in the road."

I knew it was a bit different playing goal on skates than it was in shoes. Another thing was that I had been a pretty fair winger, but I wasn't so sure I'd be much as a goalie. And it was all strange to me for another reason — in street hockey I didn't wear pads and I didn't have gloves. My equipment consisted of a pair of ski mittens and a pair of galoshes, and the kids weren't supposed to lift the can or ball or whatever. Now I was up against the hard rubber puck, and they'd be lifting and everything. Still, I said I'd do it, and to my surprise I did well enough to try it again and again. Finally I became the regular goaltender on our team and never played forward again.

My dad was tickled that I had made the move, but my mom wasn't too happy about it. In road hockey the worst that could happen was that somebody would accidently lift the puck, and I'd wind up with bruises around the ankle and shins. But now that I was playing goal on the ice hockey team, I'd come home sometimes with teeth missing or with cuts and bruises.

But my father prevailed and, at Christmas, he bought me all the goalie equipment I needed — the thick leather pads and the gloves. Of course, I didn't give up road hockey altogether, although my mother probably wished I had. One day a fellow on the other team took a swipe at the ball in front of the net; he missed the ball but followed through and hit me in the mouth with his stick. I lost one tooth.

On the ice I was luckier, and pretty soon I began playing goal for the Victoria School, on the west side of Owen Sound. The Strathcona School was on the east side, and there was great rivalry between us. As far as I was concerned, the east side kids had all the rough nuts in town. Whenever we played them, the Strathcona kids would try to give us the business with their sticks, but we always beat them with goals; which was the main reason why they didn't like us very much.

Right about that time I got a big break that was to help me tremendously in my development as a professional. Two former National Hockey League goaltenders returned to their homes in Owen Sound and were available to give me tips. One of them was Harry Lumley, who had been a great goalie for the Detroit Red Wings and later the Toronto Maple Leafs and Chicago Black Hawks; the other was Gordon "Red" Henry, who played for the Boston Bruins.

Since Lumley lived on the west side of Owen Sound, I got a chance to see a lot of him, and all we'd do is talk goaltending. He'd tell me about fundamentals. Harry would say, "Stand up as much as possible and cover your angles. A goaltender is vulnerable when he falls to the ice." Although I was quite young at the time, that bit of advice stuck with me, and I eventually developed into what people consider a "stand-up goaltender."

Harry wasn't always around to help, so I picked up goaltending tips in bits and pieces. To help myself even more I made a point of watching any hockey game that happened to be played on any given night for miles around. Once again I was lucky because in Owen Sound there was a team called the Mercurys that played in the Ontario Hockey Association's Senior A division. That meant it was one of the better semi-pro teams in the country.

It wouldn't be an exaggeration to say that the Mercurys were one of the best teams in all of Canada at that time. Their star was a forward named Tommy Burlington, and he was a remarkable athlete. He had starred with Cleveland in the American League and with the Atlantic City Sea Gulls of the Eastern League, and all the while he had only one eye. Besides Burlington, the Mercurys had Billy McComb, who had played for St. Louis, and top-notch skaters like Jack

Ingoldsby and Pat McReavy and a wee goaltender named Bobby Gillson. All in all, the Mercurys were a wonderful team to watch, and a kid just 14 years old could learn a lot just by watching them a few times a month. Which is exactly what I did; and then I'd try to apply what I learned to my own goaltending.

After I had "graduated" from street hockey goaltending to ice hockey goaltending, I began playing Bantam hockey in Canada. That's for kids from 10 to 12 years old. It was organized hockey with lots of teams, each sponsored by some club or business in town. Once a kid finished Bantam hockey, he generally moved up to what they called the Midget division, which was roughly for kids between 12 and 15.

Winning a spot on the Midget club was very important to me since the Midgets practiced in the covered arena just like the Mercurys. Even better was the fact that we'd get a chance to practice with the big team, which was about as great a thrill as a 14-year-old like me could possibly have had. As far as I was concerned, the most exciting thing was to get on the same ice with Tommy Burlington and have him take shots at me. He must have been in his late thirties or early forties at the time, but he had more tricks in his stick than just about anybody on skates. His shot itself wasn't very hard — in fact, you could almost read the label on it — but he was accurate, and he had a remarkable knack of deking — faking-out — the goaltender.

One of Tommy's favorite plays was to cut in on the goal from the right side and then head behind the net. As the goalie would see him turning behind the net, the goalie would move to the left side, expecting Tommy to swing around the goal. But Tommy would suddenly stop short and come right back out the right side. Then he'd just stand there and wait for the goalie to turn around. As soon as the goalie would see him, Tommy would tuck the puck into the corner of the net.

In the 1950-1951 season the Mercurys had one of their

strongest teams, and I had begun practicing with them as well as with my own team. It seemed that the Mercs needed another goalie to back up Bobby Gillson, and I happened to be around. I guess they liked the way I played goal because pretty soon they asked me to travel with them on the assumption that they would make the playoffs.

To Canadians the trophy that was second in importance to the Stanley Cup was the Allan Cup, for the senior championship of Canada. In order to win it, a club first has to win its own league championship; then it has to go through a long series of playoffs with other teams until it meets the Western champ for the All-Canadian title. For me to get an invitation to travel with the Mercurys in the Allan Cup playoffs was beyond my wildest dreams, yet here I was at the age of 15, ready to go on the road with them.

Mind you, the only other time I had been out of Owen Sound was once when I was quite young. My family took me to New York City to see some baseball games. Then it was back to Owen Sound until this opportunity to go on the road with the Mercurys came along.

Needless to say, I didn't expect to play in any of the games; I was satisfied to work out with the club in practices and to sit on the bench and take in all the excitement of a real live playoff. There were so many old pros around that you couldn't help notice their pet tricks and pick up some of them along the way.

Before the Allan Cup series started, I managed to get myself in excellent shape. I was in high school at the time, playing for my school club. Besides that, there was an industrial league in Owen Sound with about eight teams of grown men and some good players. I played goal for the "Empire Stoves" team. That was good for about one or two games a week. Then there was the Midget club and the practice games with the Mercs.

The intensive playing was just fine with me except for one

thing. Goaltenders are like drummers in a band: they have a lot of equipment to lug around. Since we lived a mile away from the arena, I had to lug my two bags of equipment — more than 40 pounds — to the rink whenever I played. I really hated that because I was always carrying all that stuff around at crazy times of the day. For instance, the Midget team practiced from seven to eight in the morning, so I had to be up at six. When the game was over, I had to lug the equipment back home and go to school. In Owen Sound, there was only one way for me to get around — on foot. And there were many days when I'd be doing all that carrying when the temperature was 'way below zero.

But all the hardship paid off when the playoffs began for the Mercs, because I was in great shape to go into the nets just in case an emergency should develop; and with all those games coming up it was quite possible that I'd be needed, although I really wasn't counting on it. If nothing else, I was going to see a lot more of the world than I had before. One of our first trips was to northern Quebec, about a thousand miles north of Jonquierre, where we beat the Quebec representatives.

As things turned out, one of the teams we faced in the Allan Cup playoffs was a club from Sarnia, Ontario. Well, we were in Sarnia at the time, and I was walking around the town with some of the men on the club. Early in the afternoon some of us went to a movie (I never go to a movie or watch television the day of a game in which I know I'm playing because it might affect my vision during the game itself) and then I showed up at the team meeting.

It was then that I got the shock of my young life: the coach said he wanted me to play goal that night because the regular goalie was sick. Well, when I heard that I got good and nervous, and by the time I got down to the rink that night I was so nervous I couldn't even put my gear on straight. After all, it's all right to practice against the Seniors, and it's fine to play well against kids your own age, but this was the *Allan Cup playoffs*. Somehow I managed to get out on the ice, and I played as well as I could, but we lost, 5-2.

Nobody likes to lose — I certainly don't — but I left the ice when the game was over knowing that I hadn't embarrassed myself or let the hockey club down. It didn't seem to affect the Mercs adversely. They swept past Sarnia and defeated everybody else in sight to win the Allan Cup; and I was with them throughout the series.

Still, Senior hockey was not in the cards for me because I was just turning 15. After playing in the Midget leagues, my next objective in organized hockey was the Junior ranks, which is considered the fastest pre-professional level of hockey in Canada, the stepping stone to the pros and, possibly, the NHL.

We didn't have any Junior team in Owen Sound, so it wasn't going to be easy for me to make the jump unless I was lucky. And lucky I was. One of my former teammates on the Midget club had moved to Galt, Ontario, where the Chicago Black Hawks had an affiliation with the Junior team. The club was called the Galt Black Hawks, and my old buddy suggested that I come down and try out for the team.

Although Galt is about 100 miles from Owen Sound, my parents said it would be okay for me to audition for the Junior club. At the time, I had a great deal of doubt about whether I wanted to make the move. You see, I felt very secure in Owen Sound. I knew and liked the Senior players on the Mercs, and I had been very comfortable traveling with the big club. And of course I knew my way around the Midget team. Galt would be a whole new world, and I wasn't so sure I wanted to face it.

On the other hand, I knew that if I was going to get anywhere in hockey I had to get my apprenticeship in as soon as possible, so I took off for Galt and tried out for and made the Junior team there.

Even though I was good enough to win a berth on the Black Hawks in Galt, I nevertheless felt uncomfortable during my first month away from home. Like so many other Junior players who move away from their home towns at that age, I was very homesick. I lived in a boarding house in Galt with four other guys I played with, but that didn't help distract my thoughts from Owen Sound. In that first month in Galt, I phoned home every night just to ask my parents to get me out of there and back home again. Luckily, they didn't give in to my homesick streak.

Two things helped calm me down. I enrolled in a high school at Galt, and I had to keep up with my schoolwork; and I became friendly with my teammates and was lucky enough to have a very pleasant landlady at our boarding house.

My father was also very helpful at the time. When I called home to talk about returning to Owen Sound my mother was sympathetic to me. Fortunately, she'd quickly hand the telephone to my father, and he'd simply say, "Les, why don't you stick it out a couple more weeks?"

My father followed up his advice by driving down to Galt on weekends to see the games. We played most of our home games on Saturday nights. After a while I began making fewer and fewer calls to my folks and started to settle down into the regular routine of being a Junior hockey player away from home. Pretty soon my parents began phoning *me* to see if I was still alive!

The Galt Black Hawks were a pretty fair hockey club, but nothing to get really excited about. For me it was good because a young goalie needs all the experience he can get, and sometimes it's better to play on a mediocre-to-average team because you know you'll be tested with more shots. A goalie who gets a lot of rubber thrown at him has to improve. It's a question of either improving — and surviving — or becoming a clay pigeon that gets bombed right out of the nets. I managed well enough, but even though we gained a playoff berth, we were eliminated by a determined and very strong club, St. Michael's College from Toronto. Once again I had played at least adequately, and I was invited back to Galt the following year. I wound up playing three years there for three different coaches — Red Hamill, Bob Dawes, and Al Murray — and I learned something from each of them.

By the time I reached my third year with the Galt Black Hawks, I began to think seriously about making goaltending my full-time career. I had survived in the OHA Junior A League, against the best Junior kids in Canada and in the last two fall training camps I was invited to work out against the NHL Black Hawks.

Luckily for me, Harry Lumley was the Black Hawk goalie one year, and Al Rollins tended goal the other year. They were both excellent athletes to work with, especially at my age. That was my first experience playing with or against NHL players, and I was really awed by the whole scene, even though the Chicago club was no great shakes at the time. But they did have Jimmy Conacher and Bill Gadsby and several others who were regarded as top notch National Leaguers. There was no question that I wasn't ready for them yet, but after I started my third year with the Galt Juniors, an unusual opportunity came up.

There was a club operating in Baltimore, Maryland, called the Clippers. They played in the Eastern Hockey League against teams such as Johnstown, Pennsylvania, New Haven, Connecticut, and other teams. In the Eastern League there was a mixture of old pros and kids just out of Juniors, so the caliber of the league was at least one or two cuts above the OHA Junior A League. The Clippers needed a goaltender, and I was asked to play for them. This too was a big kick for me because now I was able to see a part of the United States that I had never seen before, and I was not even 20 yet.

No sooner had I arrived in Baltimore than tragedy struck —

but with a happy ending. The Clippers had played for years in an ancient arena called Carlin's Ice Rink. For some reason, there was an explosion there, and the rink blew up and burned to the ground. Suddenly the Clippers found themselves without a place to play home games. That was the tragedy; but it didn't last long.

There had been a lot of talk about bringing pro hockey to the southern United States, and the razing of Carlin's Ice Rink turned out to be just the lever that was needed to move the game below the Mason-Dixon Line. A modern arena had just been completed in Charlotte, North Carolina, so the Clippers were moved there to finish the season.

Nobody quite knew how the southerners would react to this new game, but as things turned out the enthusiasm was tremendous. We jammed them in even better than we did in Baltimore, and there was no doubt right from the start that hockey would flourish in the South. It really was a fascinating scene because the game would be opened to the tune of "Dixie," and they'd have pretty girls skating around in pregame ceremonies.

Personally, I could have done better from the statistical viewpoint. In 59 games I allowed 302 goals to get past me, for an average of 5.11 goals per game. That isn't the best record for a goaltender, but I was invited back to Charlotte for the following season (1956-1957), and I did quite a bit better with a 3.73 average. In any event, playing in the Eastern League was a rare experience because I was traveling all over the Eastern Seaboard of the United States, and we played a game almost every night of the week. That meant a lot of moving around, and, brother, that was as hectic an experience as any hockey player has ever had.

Despite the great distances we had to travel — sometimes all the way from Clinton, a town in northern New York, down to Charlotte, North Carolina — the Clippers did all their traveling by car. This meant the players had to take turns driving all night while others slept. It was not unusual to play a game in Charlotte on a Saturday night and then to drive 600 miles for a game in Johnstown, Pennsylvania, on Sunday.

Since we had about 15 players on the squad, the club rented four cars to carry the entire team. In a sense I got a break because we didn't have a spare goalie on the club, so the other players never asked me to do the driving. Their assumption was that I needed the rest because I was the goaltender. After our games in Charlotte, I'd get in the back seat of the car and immediately fall asleep; that is, I fell asleep most of the time. Occasionally there'd be big arguments among the players in the car over who was going to do the driving.

It was really funny because sometimes we couldn't get *anybody* to drive, and the car would just sit motionless in the parking lot of the Charlotte arena while the players argued. I really couldn't blame them half the time because the guys would be so tired after the games, they just couldn't get themselves to take the wheel. Usually, after two hours or so of just sitting there wrangling, somebody would get good and mad and get behind the wheel, and we'd take off. That also presented a problem because now we'd be late and have to make up for lost time and, inevitably, we'd get a lot of speeding tickets. Sometimes I think the State Troopers had our schedule down pat because they seemed to be lined up on the highway just waiting for us.

If the driving went well, we'd get to our destination on Sunday morning, which meant we couldn't get any sleep before game time because the Eastern League scheduled games on Sunday afternoons. As a result, our guys couldn't get enough energy to play a very tight checking game, and that meant the opposition would get a lot of shots at me. It was great for an apprentice like me, because I always needed practice.

We did have some laughs on those long automobile rides but they were not always fun and games. There were also lots of bad times when we had to take the cars over some difficult mountain roads. Once a team from Nashville had an accident on one of those highways high in the mountains, and the car nearly fell right off the edge of the road. A few of the players were badly hurt.

Charlotte turned out to be a good hockey town. The weather was warm and pleasant, and the fans were eager to like hockey. Many of them were curious about it and came out to the rink just to see what was going to happen. But there's no question that they liked what they saw, because hockey is still going strong in the South, and teams were eventually added in Greensboro, North Carolina, Jacksonville, Florida, Salem, West Virginia, Nashville, Tennessee, and several other southern cities including Richmond, Virginia.

Frankly, I thought I'd become a fixture there, but in the 1958-1959 season, I was dealt to the Toledo Mercuries of the International League, which is roughly on a par with the Eastern League as far as the quality of the play is concerned. Possibly it was because I wore contact lenses during the games, although I don't think that should have figured into the coach's thinking because it wasn't a new addition to my equipment.

I had decided to wear contact lenses during hockey games (off the ice I wear regular glasses) after my first year of junior hockey. In my second year my coach began complaining because the opposition was scoring on long, easy shots, but I was making big saves on the tougher, one-on-one breakaways. So he had me take an eye test, and that's when I started wearing the contacts. I'm not using that as an alibi to explain why the Clippers dropped me; perhaps the management figured I wasn't doing an adequate job. Whatever the case, I was dropped and wound up seeing another part of the United States. The International League had teams such as Fort

Wayne and Indianapolis, Indiana, and others around the Great Lakes area.

Obviously, I hadn't gotten any closer to the NHL, but there was always hope. The move north turned out to be something of a break for me because Toledo and Cleveland had a loose agreement, and since Cleveland was in the American League, only one step away from the top, I hoped to make it there eventually.

I did get called up to Cleveland for one game in the 1958-1959 season and allowed three goals, which isn't bad for the American League. But I was sent back to Toledo because Cleveland had a very fine goaltender, Gil Mayer. In the 1960-1961 season, my last with Toledo, Cleveland began having goaltending problems. Mayer got hurt, and the Barons tried to fly another goalie in from Canada. Unfortunately, the replacement couldn't reach Cleveland in time because his plane got fogged in at Toronto. Cleveland needed a goalie in a hurry, and I was the closest one who was available.

Our club, Toledo, was having a practice the morning that the Barons were looking for a goaltender, and by the time our workout was over, I was really bushed. Then the call came from Cleveland asking me if I were willing to report. "Sure, I'll do it," I said, and I headed straight for Cleveland to play against Buffalo, the best team in the league at the time.

I played well that night, and we beat them, 5-3, but the next day the other goalie reported to Cleveland, so I was sent back to Toledo where I finished the season. Fortunately for me, Jim Hendy was boss of the Cleveland club at the time, and he was a wonderful hockey man. Hendy remembered me and asked me to report to the Barons' training camp the following season; he liked what he saw on the basis of that one game I played.

When I showed up at the Cleveland training base, I realized the Barons still had Gil Mayer as their first-string goalie, that it would be almost impossible for me to crack the lineup. Still, I worked with them throughout the time in camp, and then Hendy made an unusual offer to me; he said he wanted me to stay with the Barons as their spare goaltender *and trainer*. The reason for that was simple enough; the AHL teams in those days didn't have enough money to afford a second goalie, but they still wanted to have one around in case of emergency. "But, I don't know anything about being a trainer," I told Hendy.

"Don't worry," he said, "we'll get you Kramer's Correspondence Course for Trainers, and that'll do the trick."

Hendy wasn't kidding either. He came up with the correspondence course, and I spent several weeks studying it. "What happens," I asked him, "if there's a serious injury on the ice that I can't handle?"

"Don't worry about that either," he reassured me. "We'll always have a doctor in the building."

That made me feel a lot better, and I took my goalie-trainer job with a great deal of enthusiasm. I was getting a chance to practice with the Barons, and maybe sometime or other I'd get a chance to replace Mayer. In the meantime, it was all very interesting because there are few people who've ever come up the ranks in hockey who have had the opportunity to train and play goal at the same time.

My schedule went something like this: I'd come out on the ice later than most of the players because I had to get all the equipment ready for the workout; and that meant skates, pads, gloves, elbow guards, and everything else for 16 men. It was interesting to see how the guys would react. For instance, if the club wasn't going well, they'd insist that I change the jerseys to change their luck.

What I missed was the skating part of the workouts. I'd be on the ice in time for the scrimmage and shooting practice; then I'd leave so that I could get the towels and soap ready for the guys when they came into the dressing room after the workout. Meanwhile, I kept waiting for my big break to develop.

I remember it well. We were playing Buffalo, and I was standing near the bench munching a couple of hot dogs (I'm a fiend for hot dogs) when our goalie got hit in the side of the head with a shot. It was obvious that he couldn't continue.

Our coach was Jackie Gordon, the former New York Rangers center, who had a dry sense of humor. As soon as Jackie realized the extent of our goalie's injury he turned to me and said: "Well, who's going to go in the nets? It's either you or me, and you have more experience than me, so I think we'll have to put the pads on you!"

So, I went in, and we got beaten, 3-1. Mayer returned to the lineup again, and I began to wonder if I'd ever get another chance. But toward the end of the season Mayer got hurt again. This time I went into the nets and immediately came up with a hockey "first." We won two games in one day.

There was a power shortage in Cleveland while our club was playing Buffalo in the third period of a game. The lights went out in the whole city, including the Cleveland Arena. We were in the third period of our game when it happened, so the game was called "on account of darkness" and scheduled to be continued at a later date. The game was replayed on the next afternoon that Buffalo came to town. We beat them in the first game, 2-1, and beat them again that night.

Mayer was injured again, but this time he didn't return immediately, so Gordon continued to use me in the nets. I played the last eight games of the season and really had a hot streak. I don't think I allowed more than 11 goals altogether. Well, by the time the regular season had ended, Mayer was recovered from his injury and wanted to return and play, but I was going so well the coach kept me in the nets.

After eight regular games, my average was down to 1.38, and all of a sudden I found myself a hero, getting a lot of ink across the country. The newspapers and the wire services heard that I had been the Barons' trainer, so they picked up on this angle and played up the fact that a trainer came out of the dressing room, put on the pads, and became a star overnight — as if I had never played goal before!

I don't deny that I had worked as a trainer. I had taken care of minor injuries during the season. For example, if a player got cut, I'd stop the bleeding and put a bandage on him until we could get him to a doctor to get it stitched. Before every game I'd take a peek at my correspondence course book just to keep sharp.

When stories started to break about the trainer-turned-goalie I tried to explain to the reporters that it wasn't as simple as just jumping out of a trainer's white suit and becoming a professional goaltender. But they ignored me and kept telling it as though I had never played goal before. They had created the story, and they wanted to stick with it.

In those days I was virtually unknown around the league except of course to my teammates and a few other fellows on other teams who only knew me as a trainer. Once when we were in Springfield, Eddie Shore, owner of the Springfield team, was walking around the side of his rink when I stopped him and asked what his theory was on goaltending. Shore didn't know me from Adam, but he loved to talk about the theory of hockey. I listened to him for about an hour, and he gave me what I later discovered was the usual Eddie Shore routine. Basically, it had to do with stance; and it didn't really matter whether you were a forward, defenseman, or goaltender. Shore's theory was that a skater should be in a sort of sitting position to give him better balance.

To prove his point, Shore used a funny ploy. He'd start off by having you get into your standard crouch. "Take your stance," he'd say. Then he'd haul off and punch you as hard as he could in the shoulder and knock you off balance. "See that!" he'd say. "You're not using the proper stance." Naturally, if you hit anyone that hard when he's not expécting it, he's liable to fall over and lose his balance. But then Shore would show his favorite position. "Take this stance, there," he'd say. His was more upright than mine, with his knees bent. Then he gave me a relatively easy shove in the same spot where he had punched me before. "See that," he said, "this is much better than your stance."

Shore didn't realize I played goal for the Barons until the playoffs, when we played Springfield. In one game we played something like four sudden-death periods — more than 125 minutes of hockey — before we beat his team, 5-4, although they had outshot us, 60-20. Shore recognized me and remembered his "lessons" earlier in the year, so he went to Jim Hendy, our owner, and said he wanted $100 for teaching me how to play goal. Hendy laughed at him.

Anyhow, I had done so well in the final games of the season and the playoffs that Hendy decided to make me his regular goaltender, and he traded Mayer to Providence. This was a terrific chance for me because now I was playing all the time in Cleveland. In the 1961-1962 season I won the Rookie of the Year award with Cleveland and began to think about making it to the NHL. I figured somebody might take a chance on me, but nothing happened. And nothing happened for the next three years. I decided that time had passed me by because there were only six teams in the NHL at the time, and all the goalies there really were great.

So I was discouraged on that level but, on the other hand, I felt lucky because I was playing pro hockey and therefore had fulfilled my lifetime ambition. I'd tell myself, "Sure, everybody wants to play in the NHL, but there just isn't room for everybody."

Whenever I'd get uptight about not making the majors, I tried to put the NHL out of my mind and to keep telling myself to be content in the American League. With each season I was getting older, and it looked like there'd never be an opening for Les Binkley. But then some people started talking about expansion, saying that the NHL would add a couple of teams, and suddenly my appetite for the majors was whetted again.

At the same time I started thinking more and more about retirement. I was married and had a family, and I had several offers to take a permanent job at home in Canada. People would ask me to quit pro hockey once and for all and to go to work for them. Deep down, though, I kept hoping that *something* would come along, so I kept telling those people that I wasn't quite ready to quit hockey. I have to admit, though, these people back home were getting to me, and I was quite close to throwing in the pads in 1966. That's when the NHL suddenly decided to expand from six to twelve teams. That really stunned me because I had thought the league would expand by adding maybe one or two clubs but not six! Now the question was whether anyone would make a pitch for a goalie who wore contact lenses and was in the upper age bracket.

Another problem was the constant threat of serious injury that confronts every hockey player and especially goaltenders. Over the years in Baltimore, Charlotte, and Toledo, I accumulated hundreds of stitches, a broken ankle, a broken nose, and assorted strains and sprains, but it wasn't until I played in Cleveland that I suffered the injury that nearly ended my career before I had even had a shot at the NHL.

It happened when Pittsburgh still had an American League club. The Barons were in town for a game at the Civic Arena, and I was in the nets, when a screened shot — one that is blocked by the bodies of several players — came at me from out of the mass. Johnny MacMillan, who later became my teammate on the San Diego team, fired the shot, but I didn't actually see the puck until it was right in front of my face.

Since I wasn't wearing a mask at the time, I ducked my head, but it was too late. The puck hit me right on top of the head, at the hairline, and I blacked out in a second. I was flat on the ice. I had to be carried off on a stretcher, and I was out for two or three hours in the hospital. I wound up with a bad concussion and a 20-stitch cut in my head.

When I returned the following year, the club insisted that I wear a protective helmet, something like the one that Ted Green of the Bruins wears now. It was a form-fitting job that covered the whole head. Because of the arena heat, it was no fun wearing that thing. It caused me to perspire, and the sweat would pour down my head and into my eyes, blurring my contact lenses. I made such a fuss about it the following year that the club agreed I didn't have to wear it. Sure, the experience was painful, but soon I realized that my American League apprenticeship would pay off.

Jack Riley had been president of the American League while I was playing in Cleveland. I must have made some kind of impression on him because Jack bought my contract when he became general manager of the new Pittsburgh Penguins franchise in the expanded NHL.

That was a full year before Pittsburgh actually entered the NHL, so Riley assigned me to San Diego, of the Western Hockey League, for the 1966-1967 season while the Penguins shaped up their squad.

Moving to San Diego that year really rounded me out geographically as a hockey player. I started out in Owen Sound; traveled a few thousand miles to Northern Quebec when I was with the Mercuries; then I took in the East Coast of the United States with Baltimore; then I played in the South with Charlotte; and finally I saw the Great Lakes region with Toledo and Cleveland.

Anyway, I was really excited because I had waited many years to make the NHL, and now I was only one season away from the real thing. So my wife Eleanor and I moved to San

Diego and had a marvelous time there. It's a beautiful city, with a magnificent new arena and a lovely warm climate. We lived right near Mission Bay in Pacific Beach, with a big swimming pool right outside our door. To a guy from cold Canada it was hard to believe that it was winter in San Diego. We were only six blocks from the ocean, and we'd go down to the water every day to watch the surfers.

Of course there was hockey to be played. As I soon found out, San Diego is one of the most enthusiastic hockey cities in the country. That helped a lot because with the warm climate of San Diego it was very hard to get into the hockey playing mood. I'd just have to push myself and be sure not to swim the day of the game because that would tighten my muscles and get me out of the hockey mood.

It had always been my practice to take a nap on the afternoon of a game. But in San Diego it was difficult because the sun always seemed to be shining through my window somehow, like it was painted on. But when I went to the rink, I went there as a hockey player, and when I stepped through the dressing room door, all that outside activity was shoved from my mind. All I thought about was playing the game, trying my best to win.

The San Diego rink was very hot as hockey arenas go, and the capacity crowds made it feel even warmer. As a result the ice would get chippy, and the players had a little trouble skating and passing; but that was just a minor problem. All that I could think about was making it to the NHL and facing the best.

I played hard for San Diego, and even though we didn't have a very good team, the guys never gave up. When the season was over, I still had my body intact and looked forward to the first year in the NHL. At the time, Pittsburgh owned two goalies — me and Roy Edwards. Neither of us had had any NHL experience, and I guess Jack Riley worried about that. Before the season started, he swung a deal, trading Edwards to Detroit for Hank Bassen, who had been around the NHL for a while.

Riley must have felt that I'd be the number two goalie behind Bassen, but when I finally got to the NHL, I beat Bassen out for the job, and he eventually dropped out of the NHL. It took a long time for me to get there, but when I finally did come up it was just the way I thought it would be. Big arenas, colorful crowds, bright lights. I had come a long way from Owen Sound, but every minute in the minors suddenly became worthwhile when I had made it to the big time.

"Don't think about being a Hull. Just concentrate on being a good hockey player, and everything will work out."

— *Bobby Hull*

3

Dennis Hull

Having a father or an older brother who was a star in major league hockey often can be more of a debit than an asset to a young player. Maurice "Rocket" Richard, the explosive Montreal Canadiens' scorer who is regarded as hockey's Babe Ruth, often has said that his sons Maurice, Jr., and Normand faced too many obstacles trying to live up to their father's name when they played hockey as teenagers.

On the other hand, there are those stickhandlers who have proved that they can benefit by having a relative with a big name in the game. Bryan Hextall, Sr., the former high-scoring New York Ranger forward, has proudly watched his sons Dennis and Bryan, Jr., make it all the way to the top; and Syl Apps, Jr., son of the fine Toronto Maple Leaf center of the early forties, has established himself as an accomplished center in the NHL.

But few players have experienced the pressure that befell Dennis Hull, the younger brother of Bobby Hull, the record-breaking Chicago Black Hawks left wing.

Bobby had led the NHL in scoring twice before Dennis even set foot on Chicago Stadium ice as a member of the Black Hawks in 1964. By that time the name Hull was a household word throughout Canada and in other hockey areas of the United States. Now it was time for Dennis to prove his worth with the best of the pros.

Dennis has made it clear that his obstacles were many, and he often felt so depressed about his chances that he was ready to quit. It was during those critical moments in his minor league career that Bobby interceded and encouraged Dennis to try harder and ultimately to reach the top. And Dennis did.

Dennis talked about these experiences with the authors during an interview in late summer of 1969 in a suite at the Royal York Hotel in Toronto, Canada. He had been working on his farm near Toronto and had driven to the city for the discussion.

Relaxing on the couch, the tanned, muscular kid brother of Bobby frequently flashed a toothy grin and revealed unlimited admiration for his brother's accomplishments. It seemed there wasn't a smidgen of sibling rivalry between the two hockey players from Pointe Anne, Ontario, who had done so much for the game in Chicago.

Dennis, the 5'11", 194-pound left wing, summed it up before leaving. "I guess I'm one of the luckiest guys in the world!"

A FEW days after I joined the Chicago Black Hawks as a rookie left wing in the autumn of 1964, a fan came up to me on the street. I guess he recognized me from a picture in the paper. I expected him to talk about my career and my expectations, but he said only "Hi, Dennis, how's Bobby?"

I didn't realize it at the time, but that question was to be put to me dozens and dozens of times as my career progressed. It has been a fact of my professional life that Dennis Hull has had to live in Bobby Hull's shadow. Fans think of me more as "Bobby Hull's kid brother" than as Dennis Hull.

Some people had made it very clear to me that they consider my situation very unfortunate. "Oh," they'll say, "it must be tough being the brother of The Golden Jet." Naturally, a man must make an emotional adjustment; I think I made mine very well, just the way Joe DiMaggio's brothers Don and Vince made theirs. I'm sure they realized that they weren't going to be as good as Joe, just as I realize that I'll never be as good as Bobby.

The realization came to me when we were living in the small town of Pointe Anne, Ontario, on the Bay of Quinte, just off Lake Ontario. Bobby was six years older than I. He went off to play Junior B hockey away from home when he was 12, and I recall him coming home for a week's vacation at Christmas.

Right then and there I could tell he was somebody special. He had the bulging muscles and the strong legs, and he could do magical things with a puck when he went out on the ice. He and I would team up against our two other brothers Gary and Ron, who were both older than I but younger than Bobby. Bobby was so fast and powerful that they could hardly touch the puck so naturally we'd always win. Every once in a while he'd toss the puck to me and let me carry it up the ice, but I don't think I really began to appreciate how really great he was until he started playing Junior A hockey in St. Catharines.

By that time he already showed some evidence of the booming shot he later developed with the Black Hawks. If there was one thing I wanted to do, it was to develop as hard a shot as Bobby's. So what I would do was ask his advice, which he readily gave me. "Keep practicing, kid," he'd say. "Don't stop when the season is over, but keep at it all year 'round."

So when the ice melted, I built myself a special target made of a sheet of tin and a piece of linoleum, and I'd shoot the puck at that all the time. "Don't stop there," he'd say. "It wouldn't hurt you to do what I did and play road hockey." That was just like regular hockey except we played it with sticks on the road near our home, but instead of a puck we used a tennis ball.

Bobby wasn't my only teacher. My dad, a darn good amateur player in his day, taught Bobby and me. I have to give Dad credit. It was obvious that Bobby was the star of the family — if not the world — but Dad never put me down by holding up Bobby as an example. It was great teaching, and it rubbed off on me by the time I reached the age of 12. I remember that I had to fill out a form before entering high school, and one of the questions had to do with my life's ambition. Bobby already was playing in the NHL with Chicago, and I had begun to feel a bit of brotherly rivalry.

I wrote: "I expect to play for the Chicago Black Hawks!"

It was quite a long shot. I knew that Rocket Richard had said that his son Maurice, Jr., couldn't make it as a pro hockey player because of all the pressure and the comparisons of him to his great father, and I knew it would probably be difficult for me because I was Bobby's brother. But the funny thing is that the pressure has never really developed to a point that it really got me down, although I did have a couple of close calls. That's when Bobby saved me.

Once it happened in Junior A hockey. I hadn't been playing well for two years, and I was getting pretty downhearted. When I returned home after the season, I seriously thought of chucking the whole thing and sticking to farming back home. Bobby took me in hand and gave me a good lecture.

"Now, look," he said, "you've been playing against guys who are a lot older than you. Go back next season and, watch, you'll score 20 goals."

His reassurance really got to me. Somehow the knowledge that my brother, who was already an NHL star, had such confidence in me made me feel as if I could do things I never thought I could do before. So I went back — and I did score 20 goals. A year after that I scored 48 goals and, even though I had a year of junior eligibility left, I was invited to Chicago's camp.

I can't deny that I was nervous about going to Chicago. Bobby sensed how I felt, and right at the start of training camp he laid it on the line with me. "There's only one way to make it," he said, "and that is to play your game just the way you played it in junior. Relax. Don't be uptight. Don't think about being a Hull. Just concentrate on being a good hockey player, and everything will work out."

It might surprise some people that Bobby didn't say much more than that to me as the season progressed. His thinking was that it would be better for me to develop on my own. "You don't want me for a crutch," he'd say, and I agreed with him. I can remember my first NHL game. I didn't see him until we met in the dressing room to suit up. "If you want help," he said, "come to me, and I'll give it to you, but I'm not going to push it on you at any time."

As it turned out he never said a word. Naturally, I'd go to him, especially in those early days when I was riding the bench. I'd watch his every move, and learned plenty, especially the slap shot.

The impression Bobby always seemed to generate was one of a man who didn't have a worry in the world, who never seemed concerned about his hockey. It just seemed to be natural to him. Actually, I've seen him get depressed just like any ordinary hockey player in a slump. Once, after he had gone several games without scoring a goal, he came into the dressing room and sat on the bench without muttering a word to anybody but himself. "I'm going to skate so I can get in position so I can get off a good shot," he kept telling himself, "shoot the puck, shoot the puck."

Pretty soon I began doing that myself. I'd just tell myself what I'm going to do when I get out on the ice. I'd do it quietly. I kept things to myself, and pretty soon the things that I had forgotten began to come back.

Right from the start it became obvious that Bobby and I would be leading different lives. He always is making personal appearances and is in constant demand, whereas I live in a secluded world with the hockey players. I realized that if I scored 20 goals a season I'd be doing all right. By this time, though, Bobby was getting 50 goals a year, and I know that many people wondered if this younger Hull could do anything like that. If it bugged me not to be as good as Bobby, I never realized it. I knew what I could do. I knew I couldn't skate with Bobby, and I couldn't shoot with him. There was only one thing to do: play my position, do the simple things, watch my man, and be sure he didn't score. At no time did I ever feel any sort of jealousy for Bobby — just admiration.

For example, there was the night in the spring of 1966 when he scored his 54th goal, setting a new NHL record. I happened to be sitting on the bench at the time. As soon as the red light flashed, I remember feeling my skin tingle up and down my body.

Defenseman Doug Jarrett was sitting next to me at the time and I recall turning to him. "Geez, Doug," I said, "I've got nothing but butterflies in my stomach." Jarrett turned to me. "Y'know something, Dennis, so have I."

Some people just don't seem to realize that seeing my brother doing all those super things doesn't have to bother me. I don't have to feel any negative emotions when I watch him doing things that I know are impossible for me to accomplish — like the night he made his debut in October 1968, after his contract dispute with management.

That was when Bobby threatened to quit hockey and had actually retired for a couple of weeks. The whole situation really bothered me because I knew that my brother didn't really enjoy these fusses, and it took the enjoyment out of the game for him. He's very intense about his hockey. But if the hockey was going to be a burden to him, I knew he would forget it.

Finally he came to terms with management. I remember it vividly. The settlement was made just before game time, and Bobby came down into the dressing room after most of us had been there already. He shook hands with the guys and started suiting up. The rest of us had finished, so we went out on the ice. I sort of sensed he was nervous, but nothing was said. Then Bobby emerged from the room, and when he stepped onto the ice, the 17,000 fans went wild.

They just kept cheering for minutes on end. Bobby turned red with embarrassment. The standing ovation lasted about six minutes. Finally Bobby skated over to me and said, "Dennis, I'm all choked up." I said, "Bobby, I got news for you — you're not the only one."

I'll tell you I was happy that he returned because I doubt that I'd have made it that easily to the NHL without his help, and I doubt that I would have had the confidence to stay because in my early years with the Hawks, I had plenty of self-doubt, which Bobby helped me to erase. In my first year with Chicago I scored only 10 goals, and the next season I was sent to St. Louis. I was called up for a few games and got one goal in the 1965-1966 season.

When we returned home that summer I was terribly down in the dumps again about my hockey future. Bobby has extreme sensitivity, and his radar must have picked up my depression. Just before the next season was to begin, we had a going-away party at Pointe Anne. In the midst of the shindig Bobby got up to speak. "You watch," Bobby told the folks, "this year I predict Dennis will score 25 goals for the Black Hawks."

I was embarrassed and amazed. My father, who's a real needler, thought Bobby's crack was very funny. Dad shouted, "Oh yeah, Dennis will be lucky if he's *in* Chicago." Well, the wildest thing about it all was that I began believing Bobby's words and I *did* get 25 goals (1966-1967).

Bobby and I have different dispositions. On the ice he is more inclined to take more abuse that I do. We've always been this way. He was the heavyweight champion of Pointe Anne when we were younger, and I guess everybody left him alone for the most part. I don't consider myself more aggressive because I'm his younger brother, it's just that I seem to be more susceptible to getting hit. Once in a game against Boston, one of the Bruin players cracked me right in the mouth with his stick. It really stung and, without hesitation, I hauled off and clouted him in the stomach with my stick; I think I broke a couple of his ribs. Bobby saw that incident and later he said, "Y'know, I never would have been able to do what you did."

Actually, nobody in hockey has ever done as much for the game in so short a time as Bobby has. He's so good for hockey that I really think all owners should get together, take up a collection, and say, "Here, we'll make you a millionaire; play till you're 45, and forget about a contract."

As far as I can remember, fans have never needled Bobby, never really got on his back. I can't say the same for me, and that's when I get annoyed. Being Bobby Hull's brother has not been a help to me as far as the fans are concerned. Because of our name they tend to expect much more from me than I am capable of producing. In the 1966-1967 season I scored 25 goals, but still the fans got on me quite a bit. I still don't know whether they disliked the way I played or what it was, but I know this much — they didn't like me.

In 1968-1969 I scored 30 goals, but we were in last place so just about the whole team — even Stan Mikita, who had 97 points — took a beating from the fans.

But not Bobby. I don't think he's ever received a bad press either. When the reporters come into the dressing room after a game, they all go over to Bobby. I'd say that to this day half of them wouldn't even know which one is his kid brother. That is quite all right with me. Bobby enjoys the spotlight, but I find that anonymity makes life more relaxing. I have never received any special treatment because my name happens to be Hull. I've gotten along well with manager Tommy Ivan and coach Billy Reay. Billy has been a special help to me throughout my professional career; without him and Bobby, I don't think I'd be where I am today.

By the same token I realize that at any given time I might be traded, which is something that's not likely to happen to Bobby. Frankly, I hope it never happens because I'd sure have mixed feelings about having Bobby as an opponent rather than a teammate.

Just the thought of playing against Bobby is a strange one for me. If it ever happens, I doubt that my style would change, nor do I think it would affect my future. I intend to play big league hockey until they throw me out, whether my big brother is playing or not. Bobby feels the same way; that's one of the reasons we've gotten along so well together. We share a mutual respect for each other and understand our individual capabilities.

Bobby has never displayed a "holier-than-thou" attitude toward me. If anything, by being pleasant and understanding, he's made my adjustment much easier than it might have been. I remember a game in December 1968, which epitomizes his cool and amusing attitude toward me. We had beaten the Rangers, 3-1, and I had scored a goal and two assists.

When the game was over, reporters walked into our dressing room, and, as usual, they went straight for Bobby.

One of the newsmen asked Bobby if he thought we should team up as a business partnership. "No," Bobby said, "I don't think we're going to negotiate our contracts as a team next year. Dennis is smart enough to look after his own affairs."

Then Bobby paused, like a good stand-up comic, and added with a straight face, "Anyway, what makes you think Dennis would want me?"

I laughed when I heard that. "Sure I would," I told him. "You're still family."

Kidding aside, there isn't a hint of jealousy between us. The trick is that besides being brothers, we're friends.

Good friends.

"I was a slow developer. If I had come up earlier, I might well have been sent back down."

— *Ed Van Impe*

4

Ed Van Impe

Like so many established defensemen in the National Hockey League, Ed Van Impe reached the top via a long, slow climb up the minor league ladder.

The 5'11", 195-pound native of western Canada never caught the attention of the scouts in his youth because his style lacked the flamboyance of more offensive-minded defensemen.

But Ed played the game the way it is written in the textbooks, and he eventually graduated to the NHL when the Chicago Black Hawks signed him in 1966. Van Impe responded by helping the Black Hawks to first place for the first time in the history of Chicago hockey.

A season later the NHL expanded from six to twelve teams, and Van Impe was drafted by Philadelphia. He immediately proved his value. As captain of the Flyers, Ed led the infant franchise to the West Division championship.

Known for his ability to take an opponent out of a play

with his body, Van Impe is especially liked by his goaltenders because of his knack for keeping the crease clear of the enemy. Soft-spoken and articulate, Ed said that his unobtrusiveness has hurt him from the viewpoint of publicity. "But," he said, "defensive hockey has always been my style."

The authors interviewed Van Impe on February 1, 1971, in the living room of his home in Drexel Hill, a suburb of Philadelphia. He spoke proudly of his basic hockey training in the minors.

"It was," he concluded, "a very valuable education."

A PROFESSIONAL hockey player's development often depends in large part on whether or not he's properly encouraged in his youth. I got my start in the game as a six-year-old growing up in Saskatoon, Saskatchewan, Canada, in the middle of the western prairies. Saskatoon is one of the coldest Canadian cities, and that meant there was ice around from late October to late March. Plenty of ice meant plenty of hockey. My cousin Richard Van Impe — who was three years older than me — provided me with great incentive for learning the game.

Richard lived half a block away from our house, and he and I were good pals even though there was that age difference. When I turned six years old, Richard gave me a pair of his old skates. Although they were quite a bit bigger than my foot size, they *were* regular hockey skates, and, with a little stuffing inside, they were good enough for me to learn on during my first winter on the blades.

Our skating rink was right behind his house, so I used to walk over to Richard's place, put the skates on at his house, and then walk across the back alley to the rink. Like most rinks the kids used in Saskatoon, ours was outdoors and flooded when the weather got good and cold. The ice stayed hard unless we had one of the infrequent dry spells.

Sometimes the weather would get so cold we'd light matches in our boots to warm them up. The good thing about a Saskatoon winter is that it's a dry cold — rather than a wet one the way it is in Montreal — so it really doesn't bother you as much as it might elsewhere.

Richard wasn't the only one who encouraged me; my father, who is a cattle buyer in Saskatoon, was really great about it. He had been a senior hockey player in his day, and he loved to take me to games at the Saskatoon Arena where the Saskatoon Quakers played their Western League games. He also had his car available whenever I wanted to travel to another part of the city to play. Dad was good in another way. While he was always interested about my playing, he never interfered with my training at any level of my career and always left the coaching up to the fellows behind the bench. Too many fathers of young players get involved to the point of screaming and yelling at the coaches and do absolutely no good for their children that way.

Up until the age of ten, I played nothing but neighborhood pick-up hockey games. I wasn't particularly good in my early years, but I had a tremendous example in my cousin Richard, who had developed into an excellent young player in Saskatoon and who eventually went on to play Junior hockey for the Humboldt, Saskatchewan, Indians in the strong Saskatchewan Junior Hockey League. By the time I reached 10 years of age, Richard had become a star in Saskatoon hockey and this, in turn, proved to be a help to me: I got a chance to play my first organized hockey because the Van Impe name had some pull. I still wasn't a very good hockey player, but having the same last name as Richard helped me to get a start.

Having Richard around was important in another way because I didn't have any brothers, and he was like a member of our family. He'd always come over to our house and regale us with stories about his Junior hockey. In the meantime, I had started playing in a Peewee League, but it wasn't so great for me at first.

I started out playing defense, same as I play today, but I developed slowly as a kid. My skating and stickhandling were not that good, even when I reached the age of 14 and completed my Peewee career. In fact, I was just barely hanging on to a position on the team. But I stuck with it and graduated to the Midget level and played there for two years. Then things began breaking my way. In my second year of Midget hockey, I made the All-Star team, and for the first time in my career, I really began to become impressed with my development as a player.

In the fall of 1957, I tried out for the Saskatoon Quakers in the Saskatoon Junior Hockey League. Richard had already had a year of pro hockey under his belt with the Winnipeg Warriors of the Western League, and he seemed very pleased with the way pro hockey was treating him, so that made me all the more excited.

All this time I had maintained my interest in the National Hockey League the way most Canadian kids do, with radio and television. I'd listen to Foster Hewitt's broadcasts of Toronto Maple Leafs' games on Saturday night on the Canadian Broadcasting Corporation network. Hewitt had become something of an institution in Canadian homes from coast to coast, and when he described a goal by shouting *"He shoots; he scores!!"* it was like seeing the red light go on. There are few greater thrills than listening to Foster.

Because of the "Hockey Night In Canada" broadcasts, I became a Toronto Maple Leaf rooter, but my favorite player was Doug Harvey, the great defenseman with the Montreal Canadiens. His style really impressed me, he was cool in his own defensive zone, and he always seemed to know what to do with the puck when he got it. The guy achieved a maximum of results with a minimum of effort, and I liked that.

Hockey wasn't the only thing in my life during my middle teens. I attended high school in Saskatoon and was doing pretty well academically; well enough to get a scholarship offer from Murray Armstrong, the coach of the Denver University team in Colorado.

Armstrong used to visit Saskatchewan every year, looking for prospective players. He'd visit the high schools and talk to three or four guys on every team just to find out if they were interested in going to college in the United States. When it came to me, Armstrong simply made it plain what was available at Denver and asked whether I was interested or not. I've always regretted the decision I made.

I still had a couple of years of Junior hockey in front of me, and I had an off-season job with the Saskatoon Power Corporation. I was also taking a stationary engineering course so that if I didn't make it in pro hockey I could get a job with the Saskatoon Power Corporation.

When Armstrong presented me with the facts about college, I sat down with my parents and discussed the possibilities with them. We went over the fact that other kids from Saskatchewan, such as Red Berenson, had gone to school in the States. The great thing about my dad was that he never pushed me, never told me I should or shouldn't do anything. His view was that if I were good enough to combine hockey with a college education, it would be a good thing because I could always fall back on my academic degree if hockey didn't work out to my advantage. So, in a sense, he wanted me to accept Armstrong's offer. On the other hand, he did it in a quiet way and always left the decision to me. It was up to me to work things out the way I thought best.

I decided, in one of those inexplicable decisions kids make, not to go to college. Perhaps it was because I was excited about the way Richard's career was developing, or perhaps it was the thought of making it big in Juniors. Whatever it was, I decided against going to college, and the funny thing about it — in retrospect — is that I never realized at the time what I had said no to; about what I would have done if, say, I had broken my leg playing hockey and couldn't play again. In other words, I passed up some pretty good life insurance when I turned down the scholarship.

These decisions are calculated risks, in their own way, and my calculations were predicated on my making it as a good Junior player. So that fall I played for Saskatoon against teams from Flin Flon, Manitoba, Regina, Saskatchewan, and several other small towns in western Canada.

It was quite an experience in more ways than one. The excitement, for one thing, wasn't confined just to the ice. Sometimes the thrill of traveling from one town to another in those cold Canadian winters was more than the thrill of actual play.

Our transportation was confined to either a school bus or a car that belonged to somebody connected with the team. Whichever it was, it was terrible. We'd start out with five players in a car and always wonder whether we'd arrive at our destination in one piece or not because driving conditions were treacherous. If we had had a breakdown, God knows what would have happened to us. I should know because I very nearly didn't come out of that league alive thanks to the driving conditions.

One night there were five of us driving in a two-door hardtop, when a farmer driving in the opposite direction hit us head-on. All I remember is that we all went flying out of the car. I had been sitting in the middle of the back seat at the time of impact. The door flew open and I flew out of the door, did a couple of cartwheels, and landed in a ditch. It's hard to believe when I think back on it, but I was not hurt much at all. Only one guy had a bad cut, and our driver actually remained in the car through the whole mess. The car was totally demolished, and it's amazing that nothing more serious happened to anybody.

When we drove, we'd leave in the morning, drive maybe 300 miles through the afternoon, and play our game in the evening. Then we'd drive home through the night. And while all this was going on, I was trying to keep up with my school work.

Our club was owned by the Bentley Brothers, Max and Doug, great NHL players with the Chicago Black Hawks and Toronto Maple Leafs. The Bentleys owned three station wagons, which we used to transport the players. Their nephew Jack Bentley also did some driving. The Bentleys were great guys as people, but Max was an awful worrier. As coaches go, I don't think they were all that great, but I did learn some things from them.

Doug made one point with me that stuck in my mind more vividly than anything else. He said that when a defenseman backs up into his own zone while defending against an attacking forward, the defenseman should look his opponent right in the eye, without even looking at the puck. At the time the advice didn't seem all that important, but later on I realized how important the tip was and that it was one of the most significant bits of defensive strategy anybody ever taught me – to play the man instead of the puck.

I played three years of Junior hockey for Saskatoon and didn't feel particularly great about my progress until the final season, 1959-1960, when I made the All-Star team and was invited to play on an all-league team in an exhibition game against the touring Russian hockey team.

The game was played in Regina, and it was quite a thrill because we beat the Russians, 3-2, playing their rules, which differ from NHL rules in that they don't allow any bodychecking in the offensive zone. In other words, if I were leading an attack into the Russians' territory, one of their players could bodycheck me in their zone because they would be on the defensive, but I couldn't bodycheck them since I was on the offensive.

Physically, the Russians were very strong, and they had excellent goaltending. On the whole, though, their game was a bit rougher around the edges than it is now. You could tell even at that time by their equipment. After the game we met in the dressing rooms and traded souvenirs. I exchanged hockey sticks with one of the Russian players. His stick looked like it was homemade, and it was at least a foot longer than ours and very crude. They've improved considerably since then.

That same year we played the touring Japanese team, and that was quite an experience in itself because they were so markedly different from us in so many ways. Their skates, for example, were almost like Oxfords, and the players were tiny guys. They could skate like the dickens, but their passing, stickhandling, and shooting hadn't been thoroughly refined at the time. We beat them, 15-2, but the thing I remember most was the way the wee guys went bugging around that rink.

That Saskatchewan league was loaded with talent, which meant it was a good place to learn the basics of hockey. Some of my opponents included guys who eventually made it to the majors — Ted Hampson, Orland Kurtenbach, Dave Balon, Jim Neilson, and Billy Hicke. Today when I look back at those Junior teams, I keep thinking that the teams then were much tougher than they are now.

Kurtenbach, Balon, and Nielson were at Prince Albert, Saskatchewan, which had an agreement with the New York Rangers. Kurtenbach was one of the finest Juniors to come out of western Canada. He was big and tall and could do everything there was to do with a puck. My club was being eyed by the Chicago Black Hawks, although I wasn't aware of it at the time. It wasn't until after my final season of Junior hockey that I realized that the Black Hawks were interested. The Chicago management sent me an invitation to come to their training camp in St. Catharines, Ontario, not far from Toronto.

At first I wasn't sure how to react to the invitation. While I was playing Junior hockey I had been invited to the Black Hawks' minor pro camps in Calgary. I'd spend about ten days there, and then ten players would arrive from the NHL camp, and I'd be sent back to Saskatoon. We were mainly there to put in time, to scrimmage and stuff like that, until the others arrived.

The more I thought about it, the more pleased I was about the invitation to St. Catharines. If nothing else, it meant I was going to take my first trip to eastern Canada, which was a thrill in itself for a westerner like me. I flew there with five other guys who expected to turn pro, and I arrived in St. Catharines not knowing what to expect from the pros.

I had heard about stars like Glenn Hall, the goalie, Ed Litzenberger, the captain, and Bobby Hull and Stan Mikita, the young stars, but I was surprised at how pleasant they were to us newcomers. To me it was pretty strange because I had read about these guys and then, all of a sudden, I was right in the middle of them, and they were treating me as if I was an old friend.

Litzenberger was one player I'll never forget. He took all of us newcomers on a trip to Niagara Falls and just made us feel right at home. Some of us newcomers used to stand around gawking at the players, but those guys made the first move and started talking with the rookies and making us feel comfortable. They were really great — all of them.

In training camp they had us playing with somebody different every day. At that time the Black Hawks were pretty well set on defense, so I wasn't really counting on breaking into their lineup straight out of Juniors. I spent ten days at the Chicago camp and then signed my first professional contract. But I hadn't made the Hawks. I was sent to their farm team in Calgary, Alberta, in the Western League.

Naturally, I was a bit disappointed. Even though I was still very young, I did feel that I might have had a chance making the NHL; but on the other hand, I didn't mind going to Calgary because the Western League was a good one, and Calgary had some fine players, such as Syd Finney, Lou Jankowski, Ron Leopold, Norm Johnson, and Wally Hergesheimer, who had played for the Rangers and Black Hawks. My defense partner was George McAvoy, an experienced player and a terrific competitor. He'd regale me with stories about playing with the Penticton Vees, the British Columbia club that represented Canada in the world championship and won the whole shooting match.

Gus Kyle, the former Rangers defenseman, was our coach, and he was a great help to me. We had only four defensemen on the Calgary team, so Gus gave me a lot of ice time. No matter what happened, if I made a mistake or not, Kyle let me play. And if one of our defensemen was hurt, we'd go with three on the backline; so there were plenty of opportunities for me to develop my skills.

Our club was terrific. We clinched first place with about ten games to go, and I went home at the end of the season with hopes of making the NHL in my second year as a pro. Kyle had hinted to me that I really had a good chance of making it, but I was a little less certain. For one thing, I didn't think I was quite that ready; and for another, I knew that there were only six NHL teams at the time, and there just weren't that many opportunities for a kid. A lot of guys had told me that if you didn't make it the first time, you might not get another chance, so the trick was to get called up at the right time.

Nowadays it's a lot easier to make it to the NHL because there are 14 teams instead of only 6, meaning there are openings for about 18 players on an additional 8 teams. That comes to about 144 extra jobs more than we had when I started out. Today, if you're rejected the first time, there's always the possibility of a second, third, or fourth chance to make it.

My feeling then was that if I made it to the NHL, I wanted to make it at the start of the season, right from training camp, instead of being called up in mid-season for about five games. I knew that if I didn't click in those five games, I had had it! I didn't know if every NHL manager made those snap judgments, but I did know that I didn't want it to happen to me.

So, I went to the Chicago training camp in my second year as a pro, once more not knowing what to expect. I was there for about two or three weeks and even played a couple of exhibition games against NHL teams and I must admit I didn't do too well in them. After that the Chicago management shipped me off to their farm club in Buffalo, which then was training at Welland, Ontario.

I remained with Buffalo for the rest of training camp and then learned that I was assigned to that club rather than the Black Hawks or Calgary. I didn't realize it at the time, but I was going to endure five long years with Buffalo in the American League, and I would have to wait a long, long time before ever reaching the majors. Progress came slow, but I learned all along the way.

In my first year at Buffalo, the coach was Billy Reay, who eventually became coach of the Chicago Black Hawks. I played well for Billy and was on the club that won the Calder Cup, the playoff championship of the American League. My teammates were guys like Johnny McKenzie, who went on to become an All-Star at Boston, and Denis DeJordy, who has become a solid NHL goaltender.

After the Calder Cup win, Bob Wilson, the Black Hawks' chief scout, came over to McKenzie, DeJordy, and me and said that all three of us could pretty well be assured of getting a job with the Black Hawks the following season. But in June 1963, the Black Hawks traded goalie Roger Crozier and defenseman Ron Ingram to Detroit for defenseman Howie Young. That depressed me because I figured the Black Hawks were surely going to give Young the opening on defense. I went to training camp with a bad attitude. As it turned out, Young was going to be the fifth defenseman on the team, and coach Reay asked me if I would consider coming along as the sixth defenseman, which meant the last. "If you don't make it," Reay said, "you can come back."

Well, that was an interesting situation. Reay actually invited me to play in the NHL, which was my childhood ambition, but I turned down the offer because I didn't want to sit on the bench as the sixth defenseman. "No," I told Reay, "I can't hack that. Send me back to Buffalo."

To me the whole thing still sounds funny because I had been in the minors and I *should* have wanted to get up to the NHL just to see if I could cut the mustard. But I wanted more than anything to play and to improve, and it seemed to me that the best place to do that was in Buffalo.

But the following fall I wasn't even invited to the Chicago training camp. In fact, at one point it appeared that I might be playing for Eddie Shore in Springfield as part of a complicated deal involving Kent Douglas, a defenseman owned by Springfield who was traded to Toronto. Unknown to me, Toronto had drafted me from Chicago and sent me to Shore in Springfield.

One day I received a letter with "Springfield Indians" on the outside of the envelope. I had heard a lot about playing in Springfield, and I just couldn't see myself going there. I said to my wife, "Look, if it's come to this, I'm going back to school."

Since Toronto supposedly was involved in the deal with Springfield, I decided to check with Punch Imlach. He told me that Eddie Shore in Springfield did have my contract and that I would have to sign with him. He also told me that if I was good enough to make the NHL, Toronto had the option to sign me. Then he asked me, "Are you going to sign or phone Shore?" I said, "No, I don't think so."

It was a crazy thing, but I guess Imlach got in touch with Shore because the next thing I knew I got a phone call from Shore himself. I was playing golf at the time, and it was my wife who answered the phone when he called. Apparently Shore overlooked the fact that there was a time difference between Springfield and Calgary because when my wife told him I was out playing golf, he said, "What the hell are they doing — using flashlights?"

He was as sarcastic as hell with my wife and finally said, "You have your husband call me tomorrow morning." The next day I called Shore — collect! As soon as the operator told him it was a collect call, Shore refused to accept the charges.

I asked Shore's secretary, who was the intermediary on the phone, if they knew who was calling. She said she did, so I said, "Fine, you tell him that this is the last he's going to hear from me."

Five minutes later my phone rang. Shore was on the wire. "What did you want?" he asked.

I said, "You called *me* last night, and I was just returning your call."

He said, "Well, what do you want?"

"Now that we're talking," I said, "I might as well tell you that I'm not going to report to your training camp. I wanted to notify you of that. There's no way that I'm going all the way to training camp to hassle and then have to come all the way back home again. Tell me, what kind of money are you talking about?"

"Well," said Shore, "if I have to make an offer, I'll give you a dollar."

I said, "Do you really think I'm worth that much?"

The conversation ended there, and I didn't report to

training camp. I remained at home and began to worry about what I was going to do that winter. It was quite possible that I could be suspended and wouldn't be able to play pro hockey. One day, Shore called again.

"Gosh," he said, "you'd better think it over. I'll give you $500, and I'll fine you $250 for not reporting to training camp. I think that's a pretty fair offer."

I told him, "I think your sense of justice is a heck of a lot different than mine."

About a week went by, and I was worrying even more what was going to develop, when I got a call from the Chicago Black Hawks office. The Hawks wanted me to report to Springfield only because there appeared to be a deal in the works with Shore, and I wouldn't have to play for him after all. Well, that gave me some hope, so I packed my bags and headed for Springfield.

When I got there, I checked into the hotel where the team was staying. I got on the elevator and went up to the floor where the club was supposed to be. When I got out of the elevator, I saw first-hand what I had heard about for years: Shore had his hockey players doing dances. They were all out there — even the coach, Pat Egan — in the hallway with Shore standing in front of them doing the dance exercises.

I went straight to my room, and later I went downstairs and had dinner with the other fellows on the team. You wouldn't believe the contrast in Shore. He was a new man. He threw a great big party for the team, a training camp wind-up party, and I couldn't believe he was the same man — so belligerent at one time and so nice the next.

The next day Shore called me into his office and asked me if I was ready to sign my contract. I said, "I didn't come down here to argue."

He said, "Get your bags and get ready to go to Buffalo; you've been traded."

That wasn't my last confrontation with Shore. After that episode with the contract, our club came in to play the

Indians in Springfield. Before the game we were going through the usual warm-up, tossing shots at our goalie.

We were given two pucks for the workout, but both of them had been deflected into the stands, so we needed another one. Shore had a habit of keeping the pucks in a bucket of ice and water so that they moved easily over the surface during the game. He kept them right near the Springfield bench, a few feet away from his private box.

When we had lost our last puck, I skated over to the pail to get a replacement, and Shore saw me coming. He ran down from his private box and, just as I put my hand in the pail, he stuck his foot right into the pail of ice and water — with his shoe on. His whole foot was soaking wet. I just looked at him and couldn't believe what had happened. Eventually he gave us a puck, which we had to return after the warm-ups.

Shore was really something. Once when we were playing at Springfield, one of our players went crashing into the goalpost and tore a whole sheet of ice up. There was nothing left around the net but the cement floor. Shore wanted us to continue playing the game, but the referee called it with the score tied, 2-2, in the third period. The referee immediately called the league president and said that the game should not be continued under those ice conditions. So we went back to our locker room and began getting dressed when we learned that Shore himself had called the league president and talked him into making us finish the game. But our club had to take the bad end of the rink.

We suited up and returned to the ice — it was about 11:30 at night. We hadn't been playing for more than a minute when we scored and won the game.

As soon as the final buzzer sounded, Shore ran down from his box and grabbed the microphone for the arena loud-speaker and called the referee "a plum!" I couldn't believe some of the things he did.

I had three coaches in Buffalo — Billy Reay, Jack Evans, and Phil Watson. Under Evans we had a bad year, but it was no fault of his. Buffalo had been sponsored by Chicago, and that year Chicago sent its best farmhands to Dallas instead of Buffalo. We also lost our good center, Art Stratton, to Detroit, and we had very little talent left. We won fewer than 20 games all season and came in last place, but we had Roy Edwards in the nets, and he was terrific.

Then Watson arrived on the scene, and he was a funny guy. He demanded a lot from us sometimes and maybe he didn't always get it. But by the same token he'd sometimes turn around and do really kindly things. One year he took the entire team and the wives to the big Concord Hotel in the Catskill Mountains for four days. It was funny with Watson: one time you'd dislike him, and then he'd turn around and do something for you — really putting himself out. He was a really good hockey man but very emotional.

I believe that coaches can help a young player to a certain degree, but there's nothing that can replace *opportunity* itself. If you get the opportunity and want to make it bad enough, the coaches can help you and make it easier. But you have to have the opportunity if you want to make it.

Everyone has his one special play that he remembers most fondly. With me it was a game against Hershey in the Calder Cup finals for the league playoff championship. We had reached the ten-minute mark of the third period and were leading, 1-0, but the game could easily have gone the other way. Hershey was really pressing when I intercepted one of their passes, skated down the ice, and confronted their defense. Somehow I was able to round the defense by faking a shot and moving right in — one-on-one — against their goalie, Ed Chadwick. My shot beat the goalie and put the game on ice.

Meanwhile the years were drifting by, and after the sixth season I was completely resigned to the fact that I was going to stay in the minors. Of course, you always think, somewhere in the back of your mind, that you'd like to have the opportunity to find out first-hand whether you're good enough or not to play in the majors. But after the sixth year I began to think I wasn't going to get that chance.

In the fall of 1966 I was invited to the Chicago training camp, and frankly I don't know why they ever extended the invitation. "Look," coach Billy Reay told me, "you're going to have a chance to make the big club this year."

That was the first time anybody had ever told me that. All of a sudden the chance had come, and I thought to myself, "Dear God, I'm going to take advantage of this thing."

As the camp progressed, I was battling for the open position with a player named John Miszuk, who had been in the Black Hawks' farm system. The question of who was going to make it — John or me — wasn't resolved until two days before the end of training camp. After we had played an exhibition game against the Green Bay Bobcats, Reay came over to me and said I would be starting the season with Chicago.

A man can't ask for anything more than a chance to make good, and I was going to get that chance. I was 25 years old and was uptight. Actually, I don't think I played all that well in the exhibition games, but I had one advantage; I was teamed on defense with Pat Stapleton, who really can move the puck out of his end of the rink. Since my weakness is my offensive game, Pat complemented my game, and we worked out pretty well. He moved the puck, and I played the man a little more and blocked a few more shots.

And even though I was a bit off my game, I genuinely felt that I was ready for the NHL. I was a left-handed shot playing right defense and there was a shortage of right defensemen, so I was all set for the big time. The only thing remaining was actually playing the games.

I played my first regular NHL game at the Forum in Montreal. The score was tied, 3-3, at about the 14-minute mark of the third period; the puck came out to me, and I took a whack at it. Once I shot the puck I couldn't see it for all the players around the net, but the next thing I knew, the red light had gone on and I had a goal in my first NHL game! We wound up taking the game, 5-3.

The next night we went into New York and beat the Rangers, so I figured I was starting the season off right. We finished first that season with seven or eight games remaining, and I was a part of the club.

I owe a lot of thanks to Billy Reay, who coached me that year and helped me to develop. He was soft-spoken, but when he spoke he had a point to make, and I discovered that he made a lot of sense.

Sure it took me some time to reach the NHL, but all that minor league experience helped me; now that I have made it, I think it'll help me stay a few more years. If I had come up to the majors earlier, I might well have been sent back down. Looking back, I feel that those six years in the minors were worth every minute of it.

"Success is sweeter for having been hard to get."

— *Nancy (Mrs. Jean) Ratelle*

5

Jean Ratelle

Jean Ratelle, high-scoring center for the New York Rangers, was born October 3, 1940, in Lac St. Jean, Quebec. A smooth skater and an exceptionally gifted stickhandler, Jean has been compared to the great Montreal Canadiens' captain Jean Beliveau. Ratelle has been on the top ten list in NHL scoring for four seasons.

Jean has a league-wide reputation for being shy and reticent, but he is in fact an amiable and willing talker. The 6' 1", sandy-haired father of two lovely girls has the remains of a very strong French-Canadian accent. In the off-season, Jean is a golf pro and confesses to the truth of the rumor about his avid interest in the stock market.

Many young men coming from the Junior leagues of hockey spend several seasons in the minors before the chance comes to step up into the NHL. Jean's story is somewhat different: because of his excellent record in the Junior ranks, he immediately moved up to the New York Rangers. Then he

77

had the misfortune to be sent back down into the minor system. His story is one of reaffirming his ability.

The interview with Jean took place on a cold, sunny December afternoon in the Ratelle home on Long Beach, Long Island, not far from New York City. Jean had finished practice that morning and was comfortably relaxed. His youngest daughter, Carolyn, played around us during the interview, and his attractive wife Nancy sat nearby and added an occasional comment.

I·WAS born in the small French-Canadian town of Lac St. Jean, which is about 300 miles north of Montreal. I left Lac St. Jean for Montreal when I was ten years old, so I can't remember too much about it. But this much I can remember: it was very, very cold in the winter, and the winters were very, very long. So nearly everybody played hockey at some point in his life.

I was probably about five and a half years old when I first put on skates. It sticks in my mind because I guess the way I learned to skate doesn't happen to most kids.

First of all, I didn't start by skating on a pond or rink. No, I simply went outdoors to the nearest patch of hard snow or ice and skated. And the skates I wore were probably size ten or more — on a five year old! They were my father's skates, and I just wore them over my socks, shoes, and galoshes, all at one time, so that they would almost fit. You always hear about how important it is to have your skates fit well and how you need good support for your ankles when you begin to skate. I guess wearing the skates over my boots gave me the support I needed because I don't recall having much trouble. Nobody ever really taught me, but I don't remember falling down much.

We had no organized hockey in Lac St. Jean; we just threw the puck on the ice and played among ourselves, not as a team. We skated on a rink that was made each winter next to the school, and there was a lake nearby which we also used. I loved to skate and play hockey from the beginning, and I didn't care whether it was a rink or a lake, as long as there was lots of playing. We'd go out on the lake every day and just play for hours and hours.

I can't think of anyone my age from Lac St. Jean who went on to any kind of pro hockey, probably because there was no real organized play or coaching. There were some really fine players among my friends, though, since the long winters gave us a chance to get really good at the game.

Lac St. Jean was a completely French community, and I spoke nothing but French. Oh, I guess there were some English-speaking tourists up there during the summer and fall, hunting and fishing. But I never had any reason to associate with the tourists, so my entire world was French.

When I was ten the family decided to return to Montreal. My father — he's a dentist — had come from there originally, and I guess they just decided to go back. We had a big family, with eight kids. I have three brothers and four sisters, and there's not another hockey player among them!

We moved to the central area of Montreal, and our first year there I went to public school. I didn't like it too much because they had no real hockey teams, so I couldn't play much. I would just practice by myself at the nearest rink. I was pretty much alone and didn't know many kids my age.

The next year I boarded at Academie Roussin. There are several French-Canadian Catholic schools in Montreal. They go from the first grade to the Canadian equivalent of high school graduation. For children who live in the district of the "college," as it is called, the school is free. But for parents who live outside the district, there is tuition and board. There were more than 700 students at Roussin Academy when I arrived, and more than half of them were boarders like me.

The school was dormitory style, and it proved to be a good

experience for me. Kids are very dependent on their parents for everything, and the boarding school taught me a little about being on my own — which is particularly useful later on in a hockey career.

And there was strict discipline at Roussin, which was good for me too. It's a little like going in the army, I guess. The Brothers were pretty strict. You couldn't just walk out of the school and go to the store, for instance. If you wanted to go somewhere, you had to ask for permission. I guess I must have got caught out of line a couple of times while I lived at Roussin, but I was pretty happy doing what they wanted me to.

The reason I was pretty happy was because I got to play lots of hockey. There was a team for every grade, and for the boarders there was a league that played three or four games a week. At that time I met a kid from the district named Rodrigue Gilbert, and we became great friends, and we have remained so to this day. Rod and I played on a line together at Roussin and later on Bantam and Midget teams.

We played our Roussin league games on one of those half-and-half rinks, where there's a roof of sorts to stop the snow but no sides and no heat. It got terribly cold in Montreal sometimes, but we usually played nearly the whole game, so we didn't sit still long enough to get frostbite.

One year in the Bantam league, Rod and I were on a championship team that got to play at the Forum. We had won the district championship and then had gone on to play every other school district in the city, until we finally wound up at the Forum. It was probably the high point of my life, even though we ended up getting beaten, 5-3. Rod and I were the only fairly good players on our team, and the opposition was too well balanced for us. But it sure was a thrill. We were only twelve years old and bug-eyed to be in the place where our heroes played.

It's funny that I can't remember any of my coaches at

Roussin in Bantam or Midget. We had some good teams and seasons, so I know some of them did a pretty good job. But every year at Roussin we had a different coach: one Brother would do it one season, and the next season it was another Brother. We picked up the basics of passing and stickhandling but not too much on good positional play.

After you reach a certain level in hockey, it's necessary to learn from real pros. And there were no pros around, no so-called "power" skaters. There was nobody to say to me, "Look, here's how you *really* do it." It was next to impossible to get to the Forum to see the pros, and all of the pros who lived in Montréal were gone during the hockey season and returned only during the summer, when there was little ice. There was nothing like the hockey clinics and schools they have today for kids, so I didn't have the contact until I turned pro myself.

In my mid-teens I played for two organized teams, a Junior, or intermediate, league team at Roussin and a Junior B team with the city. The New York Rangers had a scout named Yvon Prud'Homme (which means "wise man" in French), and he heard about me from Rod. He signed me to a Junior B contract in 1956, and at age 15 I became the property of the Rangers, as I have remained to this day.

The year before Prud'Homme signed me, I had missed the entire season of hockey because of a lacrosse injury. I played center in lacrosse at Roussin, and that season I had broken a bone in my hand. It was little, but it took a long time to heal — like that bone Joe Namath broke. That injury and a broken nose at age nine were the only injuries I had until I had been in the NHL for several years. I'm never going to win any beauty contests because of that broken nose, but it's almost as if I led a charmed life until my back injury in the NHL years later. But that one made up for all those lucky years in the juniors and minors — that one almost finished me.

I played one year of Junior B hockey in Montreal for Mr.

Prud'Homme, but that whole year I wrote my good friend Rod, who had gone to Guelph, Ontario, to play Junior A hockey. I really hoped to end up there with him, but I guess I needed that Junior B experience. I lived at home with my family that year, my tenth grade at Roussin, played Junior B hockey, and dreamed of playing Junior A.

The next fall, when I was still just 17, I got the chance to try out for the Guelph Biltmores Junior A team. My father was happy that I got the chance, but I think my mother was a little shocked. During all those years I had boarded at Roussin I guess it never dawned on her how much hockey I had played and how involved I had become. She didn't really say anything at the time, but a few years later, when a younger brother of mine was really getting good at Junior B hockey in Montreal, my mother put her foot down and told him to stay in school. So I know now that she was upset that I had gone to Guelph, ending my schooling at grade 11. I tried to continue my schooling at Guelph, but it was an all English school; since I had never really spoken the language very much, it was just too tough, so I dropped out.

The language was a real problem all the way around, at first. There I was in a city of maybe 50,000 people, and for the first time in my life practically no one spoke French. Of course Rod was there and a couple of other French guys — like goalie Gilles Villemure and Marc Dufour — were on the team, but we didn't room together, and I had to fend for myself at the boarding house. As a matter of fact, our coach, Eddie Bush, deliberately roomed French players with English players so we'd learn the language quickly.

After about two months down there I met Nancy, my wife, and she began to teach me English on weekends. She was only 16 and still in high school, but she was a great help.

Rod helped a lot to make me understand what life was like down there. And even though language was a problem, my main difficulty was making the team. After all, I had come down there to play hockey, not to become a linguist. And once I made the team, I had to worry about staying there. The Junior A system is a lot like the pros in that respect.

As I said, Eddie Bush was our coach that year, and I was terrified of him. He was a former NHL defenseman, and he was loud, mean, and tough, about 6'3" and more than 200 pounds. He believed that we should build up our endurance, so he made the whole team walk to and from practice. Except for road games, he never let us ride anywhere. And he used to practice us hard. But he was a good coach because if you ever want to make it in pro hockey, you have to work really hard in Juniors.

Rod had told me all about Bush, and I have to admit that I used my language problem to defend myself against his temper sometimes. Every time he would get good and mad at me for anything, I would just stand and shake my head to let him know I couldn't understand. Of course, at first it was true that I couldn't understand him, but I could sure tell he was mad, and I'd just stand there. He'd get madder and madder, and then he'd turn to Rod and yell, "Rod, you tell him what I mean." And Rod and I would just look at each other and shrug. Bush was funny when he got mad, but he scared me too.

I found it tough to make the team that first year in Guelph. Because I was French and communication with the other players was difficult. I just didn't play regularly that first month. There was a lot of competition for center; two good English kids besides me competed for the position. So I played several games on the Guelph Junior B team that first month. Then a Junior A center got injured, and I went in for him. In my first game I got two goals and three assists, and everybody on my line got five points, so that did it. From then on Bush didn't seem to care whether I understood English or not!

Another funny thing about Bush was that in addition to

being a yeller, he was a whistler. He used to give out these terrific whistles right in the middle of a game whenever he wanted to get somebody's attention or to correct something. One of our players was so terrified of Bush that he'd stop dead in the middle of play whenever Bush whistled!

By mid-season we were doing very well, and I really began to enjoy living in Guelph. Of course, whenever I went back to Montreal to visit my family for holidays, my English suffered for a while afterwards. But each time I came back, the English got easier. And Guelph is mad about its Junior hockey. In a town that size nearly everyone knows the players and recognizes them on the street. The company that sponsored the team was the Biltmore Madhatters, a hat company, and we all wore our "Madhatter" jackets on the street. But there is good reason for the pride Guelph feels about its hockey teams: players such as Eddie Shack, Bill Sweeney, Andy Bathgate, Dean Prentice, and Ron Stewart have played for Guelph, just to name a few.

And the boarding system for players is really good for kids. We didn't really stay in a boarding house. Two boys are placed in a private home, and that family becomes almost a substitute for your own. Mr. and Mrs. Nicholas, the couple who took care of me, were really good to me. We were so busy with hockey that we didn't get too much time to socialize with them, but to this day Nancy and I still receive cards from them and their children. We kind of think of them as an aunt and uncle.

Junior hockey is where you begin to learn how to set up offensive and defensive plays. The kind of play at that age wasn't a rough brand of hockey, as you see in the pros. It was just setting up plays and trying to score goals, not that hard hitting you find later. We played 48 games in our Junior A schedule, about 16 games more than we played in the Junior B schedule. And in Junior A we practiced every day and traveled to other teams' home arenas, which we didn't do in

Junior B. In fact, in those days in Junior B, the whole team practiced together only about twice a season. I think that has changed today, and Junior B is now a much stronger league.

But at that time Junior A was just like the minors with the exception of the shorter schedule and a little less roughness. We even got expenses and boarding money, which seemed like a lot at the time. I guess we must have gotten about $25 a week for boarding and another $20 or $25 for expenses. I even saved a little bit! After all, it only cost me fifty cents to take Nancy to a local dance or a movie.

During my second and third year at Guelph, Rod and I continued to play on a line together, and during our third year I think we really had the best team in our league; without injuries we would definitely have gone all the way to the Memorial Cup. But Rod got hurt. Then two of our other defensemen, Al Lebrun and Mike McMahon, were injured, and we were left with only two defensemen, one with a year's experience and the other a rookie, so we were beaten by St. Michael's.

Eddie Bush was not my coach during my entire Junior A career; Emile Francis — who was once an NHL goalie — coached my last year. I remember sometimes we'd ask him to go out for a few shots, and he'd put the pads on, go in the net, and we'd shoot on him. It's not every coach who'll let you take shots on him! Emile has always been the same, even though he's acquired an even greater knowledge of the game since I first met him in Guelph. He's been a coach or a general manager since he was about 24 years old, when he was the general manager of a baseball team somewhere around New Battleford. He was sure a lot easier to work for than Bush, even though he was strict and made many rules to follow. But he definitely wasn't a hollerer like Bush!

In my second year of Junior A, a couple of interesting opportunities came up. In addition to my hockey, I also played a lot of baseball, mostly in left field. When I was 17, I was given a chance to sign a contract to play baseball with Milwaukee and to go to their training camp in Waycross, Georgia. I was really excited to have a chance at major league baseball. But as it turned out, the hockey season extended three weeks into baseball training camp, and that particular year I had the chance to go up to the minors and play a few games at Three Rivers, a Rangers farm team. When I had to make the choice between baseball and hockey, it was hockey.

We had already been beaten that season in the Junior playoffs, so our season was over. The Three Rivers team, though, had five or six games left until playoff time, and they wanted to make sure they made it. So Rod, Bob Cunningham, and I were sent there, and we did pretty well. We got a couple of goals and a few assists and helped them make it. I played only one game because the guy I replaced came back, so I watched from the bench. But Rod played two more games; then Three Rivers was finally defeated in the Playoffs by the Montreal club.

It was really strange to go back to Juniors after a glimpse of the pros, but it had been a good experience. Besides, we made more money! We got paid pro salaries for those games, so we jumped all at once from about $50 a week to $50 a game, plus all of our expenses. We got to travel too; we went to Sault Sainte Marie, Sudbury, and Montreal for those few games with Three Rivers.

After my last year of Juniors, I was invited to Rangers training camp in Guelph, and that was certainly a different kind of experience. Here I was among the real top players. I had a little trouble signing my contract with the coach, Muzz Patrick, that year. I had come out of Juniors one of the top players; I tied the league lead for assists my last year and made the All-Star team. I had heard that Toronto players like Dave Keon and other guys had gotten a lot of money from their organization. So I sort of figured, why shouldn't I get the same? We had to hassle a bit, but I finally got what I wanted — which means I couldn't have been asking too much!

Well, I made the team that season and played 31 games with New York. That was the 1961-1962 season. After Christmas they sent me down to the minor pros, with the Kitchener-Waterloo Beavers. I had begun to get pressured about being more aggressive, a pressure that I kept getting in New York each time I went back up. But they were losing in New York, so I guess somebody had to go.

I'll tell you, it was nice to get away from that pressure. Besides, Kitchener was near Guelph, and Nancy was still there. Red Sullivan was the Kitchener coach. We traveled a lot, to Sault Sainte Marie, Sudbury, North Bay, and Kingston. And we traveled by bus all the time, so it was pretty comfortable.

I was tired when I got sent down; my weight was down, and I was even kind of sick. When you play in Juniors it's pretty cold, and you get used to that. Then you go to a big warm rink like the one in New York, where there are 15,000 people heating the place up, and it's hard work. I just felt weak and tired. I wanted to be in the NHL really badly, but I got benched before I got sent down, and the team was in last place by that time, so it was almost a relief to be sent down. I managed to get 39 points for 32 games during the rest of the season in Kitchener, a big improvement over the 12 points in 31 games I had scored for the Rangers.

The next fall I went back to Rangers training camp again, and I once more made the team. I think Emile was taking care of practices that year, and Muzz was coach. That season I played 45 games with the Rangers — quite an improvement, no? And I thought I was having a pretty good season; I had 11 goals and 9 assists for 20 points — and that was when it was still something to have a 20-goal season. But the team was losing, and I was playing the third line, so down I went — this time to the Baltimore Clippers. I really felt that I was being blamed for the team's problems. You can't help but feel bad when you're sent down like that. You just haven't been successful, period. You don't know if you're going to get another chance. I remember I wrote to Nancy that Baltimore was a big dirty city, and I hated it, but I think she realized that I was just taking out on Baltimore what I felt about New York at that moment.

When I went down to Baltimore that first time, Johnny Crawford was the coach. Johnny was a very nice guy; he let me play my own style without pressuring me. I made another 11 goals in the few games I played there, and I think they would have missed the playoffs that year if I hadn't been there. We played the last game in Cleveland, and we *had* to win it. Quebec was just waiting for us on the sidelines. We won it in overtime, 6-5, and I had a goal and four assists that night.

We would often play Friday, Saturday, and Sunday night games in a row, traveling all the time by chartered buses. The schedule would have been murder, but the kind of game we played simply wasn't as tough as those in the NHL. The competition just wasn't as strong, nor were the players quite as good. I could go into Baltimore and virtually be a star, but I hadn't been able to make it in the NHL. I didn't feel that there was that terrible pressure on me that I had suffered in the NHL. Besides, down there I took my regular turn and got to play the power play, so I was getting used a lot, whereas in New York I had to go up against competition like Andy Bathgate and Dean Prentice — it was too much, too many big guns.

The next fall I made the usual trip to Rangers training camp, that time in Winnepeg. I had a good training camp, too, but this time, as my luck would have it, they got Phil Goyette and Donnie Marshall. That was the end of me right there. So I started the season in Baltimore, and in a way that was reassuring. At least I knew where I stood right off the bat. Aldo Guidolin, a good defenseman who should've made it in the NHL, had started coaching the Clippers that season, and he was always good to me. He has remained a good friend of mine ever since those days. He was always fair, and I really tried to do my best for him. He would work with us individually if we needed it, but he was greatest on coaching teamwork and team techniques. He was the type of guy who would always say to me, "You just keep working, and you'll be back up there (meaning the NHL)." He gave me the ice time I needed, and he never pressured me to play a style of game I hadn't been brought up to play.

I've been told since those days that Aldo has said you shouldn't force a French-Canadian player into an aggressive style, that they're stickhandlers and puck carriers and can't be forced into aggressive, hard-hitting play. I think he's probably right on that. Most French boys go to some kind of "college" to learn their hockey. They're not really allowed to do any real fighting or hard hitting on the ice. This may have changed since I went to school, but that's the way it was in my time. And we weren't really taught to hit. If that's what you're taught when you're young, that's what stays with you. If a player is going to learn to be a hitter, it has to be instilled in him when he's young.

Part of molding young French players, too, is their looking up to the Montreal Canadiens as models. They had the really great teams when I was a kid, and every French boy wanted to be like the Canadiens. We all looked to those who got the goals, carried the puck, made the most points — not who fought the best.

As for my basic style, I know that as I matured, people began to compare me to. Jean Beliveau, the great Canadien's center. This is very flattering, but I think it's basically because we're French, tall, similar skaters, and we're both centers. I never consciously modeled myself after him or anyone else. We never had the same coaches or played for the same teams as kids, so any similarity is just coincidence.

As for the skill of stickhandling, I honestly think that no

one person taught me that. Many coaches through the years taught me how to receive a pass and things like that, but the basic skill is mostly a question of whether you have it or you don't — and you usually learn that on your own at a young age.

Regardless of how much confidence I might once have had, however, by the time I went down for the third time, I had begun to believe what they had been telling me in the NHL about being more aggressive. I really tried to be more hard-hitting but I have never been a fighter. And I do think that when I finally did make it back up for good, I was more aggressive, at least about going in the corners and digging out the puck.

That last season in Baltimore was a good one for me. I had 20 goals and 46 points in 57 games. We were a good team. Nancy and I were married by that time and we liked Baltimore. It had a pleasant climate, and I got to play a little golf during the season down there. I was still pretty much of a youngster compared to a lot of the guys, but they never treated me like a kid. Noel Price, an old vet, was there, and Dave Creighton and his wife were our best friends. He's 11 years older than I, and I think that was his 16th year in the pros. Age doesn't matter in a situation like that; it's simply a question of knowing that we're all in the same boat.

Even though I guess I was being watched pretty closely to see if I would be capable of going back up, I didn't have any feelings of competition with the rest of my teammates. Bryan Hextall was there, and he had been brought up a couple of times too. But when we were in Baltimore, all we worried about was the team. I couldn't have cared less about New York. I knew I had had my chances and hadn't made it, so I was trying to forget. Oh, sure, I was young, and I thought that maybe in another year I might get another chance. But at least at the beginning of that season I knew where I was going to be — in Baltimore. All I could do was improve.

I know that I've always had a reputation for being quiet, but I feel that during my stint in the minors I developed into somewhat of a team leader. It wasn't so much that I could give the team a pep talk before the game or anything like that; rather, it was because of my style of play. If you just do your very best as consistently as you can, it does something for the whole team, and that's a lot of what I learned down there, particularly with Aldo.

After 57 games with Baltimore that year, there was a big trade in New York — the Bathgate trade, when Arnie Brown and Rod Seiling and the Toronto boys came to New York. And they decided to bring me back up to finish the rest of the season playing with Bob Nevin and Dickie Duff. It was only a few games, but I did pretty well this time, and I figured if I could just continue to play with those two fellows, I'd make it with the team. And I did.

As I look back on my experiences, I realize that there are a couple of myths about hockey and the minor leagues. The first myth is that all Canadian boys play hockey and dream of being an NHL star one day. It's true that Canadian winters are long and cold, and there are few boys who aren't exposed to hockey to some degree, but today there are many Canadian boys who don't consider for a minute being professional hockey players.

The other myth is about the grind, sweat, and hard work of the minors. Sure, the whole thing is hard work, but you have to remember that the first reason that most guys go into professional sports is because it's *fun*. I have played nearly all sports — including baseball, lacrosse, hockey, even some basketball in high school — and to this very day, hockey is the most fun for me.

As for the grind and work, I think that having minor league experience was invaluable to me. When a kid is young and coming right out of Juniors, he would be a lot better off in the National League one day with one or two years' experience in the minor pros. I would go so far as to say that most guys *have* to have that experience. It's the rare athlete — like a Bobby Orr — who can come right out of Juniors and play his best. There isn't enough opportunity in the Juniors to have contact with the tough pro hockey players. I can't put my finger on any one lesson or player that really gave me something special to take to the National League. The entire experience gave me a kind of confidence I could draw on later.

Nancy and I did sweat those years, believe me; but it means more somehow than if I had stepped out of Juniors and skated immediately to stardom. It's like Nancy says: "Success is sweeter for having been hard to get."

"I had a lot of rough edges that needed smoothing out."

— *John Ferguson*

6

John Ferguson

Those who remember John Ferguson as a minor league player in Fort Wayne, Indiana, and Cleveland, Ohio, still find it hard to believe that he ultimately became a major league star for hockey's greatest dynasty, the Montreal Canadiens. "He couldn't skate," said Jack Gordon, his coach in Cleveland, "and he couldn't shoot. But he sure could work hard. That's why he eventually went all the way to the top."

The odds were against the 6', 190-pound left wing right from the start. He grew up in Vancouver, British Columbia, where natural ice is a rarity, but he loved the game so much he finally got himself a skating rink job, enabling him to put in many hours of skating practice.

He also got himself a job as stickboy for the Vancouver Canucks professional team, and he got his first lesson in hockey's jungle warfare by watching a battle in front of the Vancouver team's bench. Ferguson saw Edmonton defenseman Larry Zeidel batter Vancouver forward Phil Maloney while the Canucks players looked on without helping their teammate.

"Not one guy went to help," Ferguson recalled. "I hated that whole team and made up my mind that if I ever became a hockey player, I'd never stand by and watch something like that happen to one of my teammates."

Years later, when Ferguson was playing for Cleveland and Ziedel, for Hershey, the two clashed. "I gave Larry a few for Phil," Ferguson said.

Ferguson's march through the minors was impeded by battles. Once Gary Collins of Pittsburgh questioned John's toughness. "I'm tough enough to handle you," said Ferguson, and he pushed Collins against the players' bench gate, knocking it open.

Ferguson reached the NHL in 1963, but he never stopped battling. During the Stanley Cup playoffs of April 1968, it appeared that the Boston Bruins would attempt to intimidate the smaller Montreal Canadiens. At the time, Ted Green was the presiding Boston bully. Ferguson stopped Green in a trice at the start of the series, and the Canadiens easily won the playoff round and the Stanley Cup.

A part-time horse racing columnist for the Montreal Gazette, *Ferguson is the epitome of etiquette off the ice. We interviewed him twice — in November 1969 in the dining room of the Warwick Hotel in Philadelphia and in January 1971 in his room at the Statler-Hilton Hotel in New York.*

He spoke intensely of the game at which he has worked so hard, and his voice became almost melancholy when he considered how expansion had made it so much easier for the kids of today. "I watch some of our younger players," Ferguson said, "and see lots of talent. But I also see that they don't want to work at it as badly as we did, and it makes me sad."

M Y UPBRINGING was quite a bit different from that of the average Canadian who eventually makes it to the National Hockey League. I was born and grew up in Vancouver, British Columbia, on the western coast of Canada. Unlike colder places such as Montreal, Winnipeg, Saskatoon, and other hockey hotbeds, Vancouver has a relatively mild climate. That means that there was almost no natural ice for me to learn to skate on as there is in other parts of Canada.

I grew up in a section of Vancouver called Hastings East, where the big sports were lacrosse and soccer. Both sports appealed to me a great deal until I discovered that there was hockey to be played at the local arena, in a minor program for neighborhood kids. In other parts of the country the kids usually start skating when they are five or six — some when they are just able to walk, but I didn't start skating until I was thirteen years old.

A year later I enrolled in the "Bantam" league. We didn't have much money in our family, so it would have been pretty difficult for me to get all the equipment that was necessary for organized hockey. Luckily, I had two older friends — Tom McVeigh and Harold Fox — who were playing a more advanced brand of hockey. When McVeigh left Vancouver to play in Prince Albert, Saskatchewan, he gave me his old skates. Fox gave up hockey to become a plumber, so he gave me all the rest of the equipment I needed. All I needed after that to improve my skating was the ice.

In those days the biggest arena in Vancouver was the old Forum, where the Canucks of the Western League played their home games. It was an ancient place, but it did have one very good thing about it: there was plenty of ice there. When a place like that has ice, it invariably needs people to take care of it, and that's where I came in. I was one of a group known as "rink rats."

We were local kids who couldn't get enough ice to skate on to satisfy us, so what we did was work at the rink, cleaning and scraping it in return for the privilege of skating on it. I was out at the rink early in the morning until late at night, skating whenever I could.

At the Forum there were two permanent sheets of ice, the figure skating rink in the back and the hockey rink in the front. After the figure skaters were on their rink for an hour, we "rink rats" would come along and clean it off. Then we'd do the same for the hockey rink. Consequently, we always seemed to be lacing and unlacing our skates and trudging on and off the ice.

We didn't do this for nothing. There were eight "rink rats" in all, and we made 25 cents for every patch of ice we cleaned. By the end of two weeks we collected from $25 to $35. Naturally, all of this work had to be done when I wasn't in school. In other words, I'd be on the ice at seven in the morning for an early clean and then again at eight and once more before I left for school at nine in the morning. At that time they didn't have the machines they do now. We'd use a squeegee — a long rake-like device with a rubber blade at the end. We'd scrape the ice and then apply a hot mop that made the ice freeze faster.

At one point, some of the guys thought we weren't getting enough money and asked for a raise, but we didn't get it. In retaliation, one of the older guys cut the water hose during a hockey game so that they couldn't get a fresh sheet of ice between periods. When the owners found out that one of the rink rats did it, we were barred from the Forum for a whole month. They used the mass ban because they wanted us to tell which guy did the job on the hose, but nobody would tell.

In the end, though, our move paid off. We wound up getting a raise to 35 cents a clean, which in those days was big money. We didn't fool around on our job because there always was the threat that somebody else would take our place. And since ice was so hard to come by in Vancouver, there always were three or four spares among the rink rats who were just aching to get the job.

Sometimes, though, one or two of us would be away on a weekend because we were playing lacrosse or soccer and we always made sure to have one of the spares pinch-hit for us. And if a guy didn't show up for some reason and there were no spares, which happened to me quite a bit, I had to do two jobs and got a "double clean." That was real work.

In my early days it seemed as if I never really got away from the Forum because in the summer I was involved with the racetrack, right next to the Forum. I'd work as a stable boy, a groom, and just about everything else that has to be done at the track. By the time the racing season ended, hockey was ready to start, so there was no conflict between the sports or jobs for me.

Hockey was played at crazy times. Sometimes we'd be on the ice at 6:30 in the morning. Right after the game we'd head for the soccer field for a game. By late afternoon our legs would be aching so much we'd be in bed by 6:00 that night. Then up at 6:00 the next morning to clean the ice and so on like that, until I became a good enough skater to think about hockey as a career.

One thing that helped me think more and more seriously about it was a job I got at the Forum as a stick boy for the Canucks. I got the job just by hanging around the rink all the time, constantly helping the trainer and the others unpack bags, polishing skates, or carrying skates that needed sharpening to the sharpener across the street from the rink.

If you were lucky, you wound up being asked to be stickboy for the visiting team. Eventually you might make it as stickboy for the Canucks. In order to keep the job you had to rule the roost because there were a lot of other kids competing for the job. It was a status thing; the kids at school looked up to stickboys and rink rats.

While all this was going on, my hockey was gradually

improving, so I decided to try and make a career of it. The last age grouping I played for in Vancouver was Juvenile, where I got an offer to play for a team in Melville, Saskatchewan.

At the time, the New York Rangers were interested in me, and they wanted me to play for their Junior team in Prince Albert, Saskatchewan. But because of the complicated rules about players being imported from another province, I was ruled ineligible for Prince Albert but approved for Melville.

So I got on a train at Vancouver and headed for Melville, which is in one of the coldest parts of Canada, the plains of Saskatchewan. I had no idea what to expect when I got there, so you can imagine my amazement when the train pulled into Melville station at three in the morning and this tall, lanky man met me on the platform. His name was Bill "Legs" Fraser and he was the coach of the Melville team. Legs had been a terrific professional goaltender in the Quebec Senior Hockey League with the Ottawa Senators and had played against some of the finest skaters in Canada.

But when I got off that train from Vancouver I had no idea what Fraser's personality was like nor did I know that he had a great sense of humor. The first thing he did after introducing himself to me was to frisk me from head to toe! I guess Vancouver kids had a bad reputation.

I didn't have any trouble with Legs after that; I had plenty of laughs with him. We never knew what to expect from Legs. One year we had a goaltender on our club by the name of Donnie Hamilton, who came from Victoria, British Columbia. Donnie always had the Victoria newspaper mailed to him from home, and he'd bring it to the rink and read it in the dressing room.

On this particular day Legs got hold of the paper, sat down and read it and then, just as Donnie expected him to return it, Legs pulled out a match and burned the paper to a crisp.

Then he gathered the ashes and put them in his shoe. Of course any heat we could get in Melville was appreciated because that was one very cold town. It was nothing for the temperature to drop to 30° below zero, and there were plenty of times when it hit 50° below at the rink. The dressing room was the only place in the rink where we could get warm.

Like most Junior players living away from home, I stayed at a boarding house with a couple of other players. The people who owned the place had a couple of extra rooms. They put us up, cooked our food, and made us feel as if we were part of the family.

Legs Fraser was a stickler for conditioning and team spirit. He worked us hard in practice, but it was worth every minute of it. And it was cold. During practices we'd have to wear regular gloves under our hockey gloves to keep our hands from getting frostbitten, and we'd wear heavy scarves around our necks. It may not seem very important, but we had to be extremely careful to make sure our socks were dry. If we put on wet socks, our feet would freeze, and we'd be in big trouble.

Of all the bunch, Legs seemed to take to the cold the best. He'd put up with the coldest weather without a whimper. He'd walk to the rink with his police dog, and Legs had an air about him that made us admire him on sight.

Melville played in a really tough Junior league against some of the best young players in Canada at the time. In Regina, Saskatchewan, they had an awfully strong club, with Red Berenson at center. Of all the Junior players I've gone up against Red was the best. He could carry the puck, shoot, and play defensively as well as offensively; there just didn't seem to be a thing he couldn't do. Bill Hicke also was a star with Regina, and Prince Albert had Dave Balon and Orland Kurtenbach, two very fine Junior players.

Another team in the league was the Flin Flon Bombers from Flin Flon, a small town in northern Manitoba, which was quite a distance from Melville. In order to get there, we used to arrange car pools. Officials of the team used to canvass the city and the club directors for cars to take us to the road games. In order to raise extra money, the arena had a special "Car Bingo," and they used the money from that for gas and other traveling expenses.

Traveling through those bitter Canadian prairie winters was no joke, believe me. We made a point of traveling in convoy to make sure that nobody got lost. We always had to stop somewhere along the line to push somebody who had gotten stuck in the snow.

One night we were heading away from a game we had played in Estevan, Saskatchewan, when our car got stuck off the side of the road. It must have been 30° below zero at the time, and it looked as if we were never going to get the car back in shape. Finally, one of the other players and I started walking along the road, looking for help. Eventually, we came upon an old farmhouse with some lights on, so we knew there were people in there.

We knocked on the door, but nobody answered; apparently the people were afraid to open the door because they didn't know who was out there and they didn't want to take any chances. We were so desperate we kept banging on the door, and they finally yelled from inside, "Who is it?" Somehow or other we managed to convey our problem to them and to persuade the farmer to come out and help us.

The farmer went to the barn and came out with a huge horse. He walked the horse the two miles down the road to where our car was stuck. We chained the horse to the car bumper, and after a few mighty pulls the horse managed to drag the car out of the snow so that we could continue our trip back to Melville.

Another time we were coming from Estevan, driving home

without any problems, when suddenly on the road ahead we saw a car completely in flames. There was no way to get past the machine that was blocking the road since there was only one lane cleared for traffic both ways. The weird thing about that sight was that when we finally approached the car after the fire had burned out, we couldn't find a single person around the car. Nobody. There was an empty, burned-out car on a side road in the middle of nowhere. It took a bit of doing but we finally managed to drive around it and continue on our way.

There were plenty of strange incidents on the road between games. I remember one New Year's Eve when we had a game in Prince Albert. After the game we had planned to celebrate with a few beers, but we made the mistake of leaving the case of beer in the car trunk. When we opened the trunk after the game, the beer was frozen solid.

To get back to Melville we had to stop first at Regina. On our way out of that town, we broke our drive shaft, and the car was stuck. We knew that it would be three or four days before anything could be done for the car, but we had to get back to Melville, a good 160 miles away.

Somehow we discovered that the Royal Canadian Mounted Police, which traveled in patrols back and forth on the Saskatchewan roads, had just taken a prisoner in Regina and had to get him to Melville, so we hitched a ride back home to Melville with the Mounties and their man!

All in all, I'd say that Melville was one of the best places for a young hockey player to learn the game. It was a railroad town with just about everybody working for the Canadian National Railway. When we weren't playing, we were at the rink practicing; when we weren't practicing, we were shooting pool at the local billiard parlor.

When a hockey player is starting out, the coaching plays an important part in his development; much of the attitude that I carried into the professional leagues was molded by Legs

Fraser. If there was one thing he drilled into me it was the idea of fighting for your own club and not giving an inch to the opposition. He strictly forbade any fraternizing with the opposition. If Legs saw one of his players stop to talk to any player on another team, he'd fine his player right off the bat. And that was quite a penalty because a fine against a Junior player could just about break him. But Legs got his point across; after a while he got us to hate the opposition. It was a trait that I carried with me right up to the NHL.

Before my last year of hockey in Melville I married Joan, my childhood sweetheart. She had been a figure skater at the Vancouver Forum when I was rink rat there, and Joan and I went to high school together. During my first two years in Melville she skated in the Ice Follies. Then we decided to get married, so she came to Melville with me where I played my last year of Junior hockey.

Although Junior hockey in Canada is considered "amateur" hockey, the rules governing amateur sports in Canada differ somewhat from the amateur rules in other parts of the world. In hockey, an amateur player is given a certain amount of expense money, and after Joan and I got married, I was making $125 a month playing for Melville. We lived in an apartment on top of a theater and paid $72 a month rent, so we managed to make ends meet.

Like most coaches, Legs had an incentive system. He gave bonuses if a player scored a certain number of goals, and I managed to earn as much as $210 a month when I was shooting well. In 44 games in that last year of Junior (1958-1959), I scored 32 goals and 34 assists for 66 points. I was captain of the team and finished about sixth in the scoring race, so I was feeling pretty good about my chances of making it as a professional. The question was where.

There were several possibilities. For starters, I knew that the New York Rangers were interested in me. They had the Western League farm club in Vancouver, and they also had a tie-in with an International League team in Fort Wayne, Indiana. It was also possible for me to go on to college because I had been offered a scholarship to Denver University.

Making a decision wasn't easy. I had had a great desire to be a veterinarian ever since I was a kid. My father had always wanted me to be one, and I had grown up with horses and loved them. I knew them inside out and could diagnose a bad leg on a horse when I was a kid, so that was quite a lure for me. On the other hand, I had been training hard to become a professional hockey player, so I decided to try out for the Vancouver club and to see what would happen.

Well, I had a pretty good camp. I hit some of the big guys, and I figured that I was making an impression on the management. Art Chapman was running the club at the time, and he made it clear right from the start that he didn't think there was room for me on the Vancouver club. Still, I lasted with them right until the last day of training camp and then, for a while, it looked as if I would actually make the club.

A player on their roster by the name of Danny Belisle had been holding out for more money. At the time it seemed that Belisle wasn't going to play in the opening game, so the management kept me on the squad. I went with the team to the airport for the flight to Victoria and the opening game of the season. Just as I got on the plane, one of the bosses came over and said to me, "Well, son, we can't use you because Belisle signed today. We're sending you to Fort Wayne."

So I said, "That's okay; that's fine with me." I got off the plane and phoned Murray Armstrong, the coach at Denver University. "Murray," I said, "I'm coming to school." By now, everything was set for me to go to Denver except for one thing — the New York Rangers still had strings on me, and before I could make a move toward the university, Muzz Patrick, manager of the Rangers, was on the phone saying he wouldn't let me go to college. He said he had plans for me in the New York organization. The problem was that I had signed what they called "a form," which tied me to a professional team and allowed the club to prevent me from going to an American college. There was nothing I could do but report to Fort Wayne when the Rangers ordered me there.

The move to Fort Wayne was one of the best things that ever happened to me. A big reason for that was Ken Ullyot, the fellow who ran the Fort Wayne club. He was an excellent hockey man in every sense of the word — great coach, manager, and promoter. Although Fort Wayne was only in the International League, which is a cut below the American League and two cuts below the NHL, the Komets used to pack 7,000 fans into the arena on a Saturday night. Ullyot taught me all the hockey fundamentals, and he was a great one for conditioning. He had a lot of rules, but they all were sensible, and I always admired him for that.

We had a winning team in Fort Wayne mainly because Ullyot kept a lot of pressure on us. He'd set a target and expect us to achieve it. Ken was a great one for records, and it seemed that we always were shooting for one record or another. Once we set a record with 23 straight wins.

Traveling in the International League was something like it was for me in Junior hockey except that the weather wasn't as cold. The Komets traveled to road games by station wagon. Altogether we had about four or five wagons, and Ullyot usually drove one of them while the players would drive the others. Whenever we had a trip, Ken would establish a meeting point. For instance, if we were heading for Minneapolis he would establish motor lodge "X" as our stopping-off place. He'd phone ahead to book the rooms, and we'd stay there for the night. It was a first-class system for that level of hockey.

No matter where a hockey man happens to be playing in the minors, he always thinks about making it to the NHL, and that gives him the incentive to play harder. For me the incentive was there because there always seemed to be a player coming down from a higher league, which meant I constantly had to play harder and harder to keep my job.

I guess a lot of people think of the Minor Leagues as a place where you can goof off, but that's not true — at least not when you're young. I was pretty straight, and I kept trying to work up to the Western or American Leagues. The main goal was to get to the next higher level before thinking about the NHL.

It didn't take long for me to realize that if I gave up hope, I'd be dead, and I was young enough to understand that an older guy who came down from a higher league did so because he couldn't make it any longer. I wanted to get that opening.

Ken Ullyot made sure that I never goofed off. One of his policies was not to accept too many demoted veterans because he figured that if they were coming down from a higher league, they weren't winners. But he made sure to tell us that if we didn't do our jobs, there would be someone else to do them for us.

I enjoyed playing in Fort Wayne. The competition was good, and it was interesting to visit a lot of American cities I had only heard of before. That year Louisville had a team in the International League, and we played there every so often. Once when we were in Louisville, we went to see a boxing bout in town. I forget who the headliner was, but another guy on the card was a kid named Cassius Clay. It was his first big fight, and he kept going up from there.

In 68 games with Fort Wayne I scored 32 goals and 33 assists for 65 points, which wasn't too bad. The Komets led the league, and we went through the playoffs until we came up against St. Paul. They beat us out, four games to three, which was a real letdown. Personally, however, the loss wasn't a complete disaster because Jim Hendy, manager of the Cleveland Barons, and his coach, Jack Gordon, had scouted me and had liked what they saw.

Although the Rangers could have kept me in their organization, they failed to put me on their list of "protected players." That meant that an independent hockey club like the Cleveland Barons could sign me. Two teams were after me — the Barons in Cleveland and the Totems in Seattle. Hendy came up with a better offer than Keith Allen in Seattle, so I signed with Hendy. He gave me a bonus and said I would get still more money if I made the club. That was in the 1960-1961 season. I came to camp that fall and made the club along with Wayne Larkin of Winnipeg. Wayne and I sat down together with Hendy and signed the same contract: so much bonus, so much more for goals scored, and so on. Three-quarters of the way through the season, Hendy passed away and Jack Gordon took over as manager and coach, but Jack honored every agreement we had made with Hendy.

The Cleveland experience was as helpful to me, if not more so, as the one in Fort Wayne. I had the advantage in Cleveland of playing with some really excellent players, who also had a great influence on my hockey philosophy. One of them was Aldo Guidolin, a defenseman who always told me, "Never stop working, Johnny." It was good advice because I had a lot of rough edges that needed smoothing out. My skating still wasn't that good, and I had to perfect my shooting too.

I played 62 games in that rookie season with Cleveland and scored 13 goals and 21 assists for 34 points. It wasn't a record-breaking year for me, but at least it was a step in the right direction — toward the NHL. After the season I returned to Vancouver, where I did some work at the race track, played lacrosse, and ran the sports program for the boys detention home in Nanaimo, British Columbia.

The 1961-1962 season in Cleveland was an improvement for me. I scored 20 goals and 21 assists for 41 points and began to feel at home in the American League. We had a good club: we had players like Gary Bergman, Cal Gardner, and Bill Needham, all of whom played solid hockey. And of course, we had our laughs.

Playing for Cleveland meant I was only one rung away from the NHL, but that was a big rung. If I had had any doubts about it, all I had to do was to talk to one of the guys like Cal Gardner or Hank Ciesla, who had been in the majors and knew the difference. One major difference was the way the players travel. In the American League it was mostly by bus; in the NHL it was by jet. I remember Ciesla used to say, "The only difference between the American League and the NHL is the runways!"

Still, we always managed to make ends meet in Cleveland, although I certainly didn't get paid very much. The most I ever earned in Cleveland was $6,500, but I always looked on the experience as a learning process. One of the best teachers I had was Freddie Glover, who was both a player and a coach for Cleveland.

I learned just by watching Glover in action; he was the greatest competitor I've ever seen. Nothing would stop him. For example, even when he was badly hurt, he still insisted on getting back into action. He'd have himself taped up from head to foot, yet he would somehow manage to return to the ice because he loved hockey so much.

Freddie fought a lot, and he occasionally lost. I've seen him get whipped worse in fist fights than any guy I've ever seen; but two minutes later Freddie would be up and at it, going after the same guy who had beaten him up. Just being around Glover was enough to pick up another player's spirits.

In 1962-1963 I played in 72 games for Cleveland and scored 38 goals and 40 assists for 78 points. I was assistant captain of the Barons, and I was hoping that somebody from the NHL would have an eye out for me. When we reached the playoffs against Hershey I learned that Toe Blake, the coach of the Montreal Canadiens, was scouting me, and when the season was over, I learned that I had made the AHL All-Star team. I realized then that my chances were never better for moving up to the highest rung of all — the NHL.

In the springtime after the playoffs, Jackie Gordon called me into his office. "You've got a chance to go to either the New York Rangers or the Montreal Canadiens," he told me. "Where do you want to go?"

"I want to go to Montreal," I told him. "The last time I was with New York I never had a chance."

Apparently a trade had been in the works. I was supposed to go to the Rangers with goalie Les Binkley and Hank Ciesla, and goalie Gump Worsley and forward Ken Schinkel were to be sent to Cleveland in return for the three of us.

But I told Gordon, "Ever since I was a kid I've wanted to play for the Canadiens."

I never quite figured out how the original deal was unscrambled and how I wound up going to the Canadiens, but a season later Montreal launched a working agreement with Cleveland and began sending a lot of their good young players to the Barons.

Needless to say, going to Montreal was the biggest thrill imaginable because it fulfilled my life-long ambition. When I got to training camp that fall of 1963, I had no idea whether or not I would make the big club, but I was sure going to give it a try.

The first thing I did when we started scrimmaging was to run into as many opponents as possible. That seemed to please coach Blake, and I managed to survive every cut in the squad. I finally learned that I had made the team.

Blake started me on the left wing with captain Jean Beliveau at center and Bernie Geoffrion on right wing. We opened the season at Boston Garden, and I scored two goals and one assist in my first NHL game. It was incredible. After that, there was no looking back.

In retrospect, I always have believed that the minor league experience I got was invaluable. I think that if you work hard in the minors and finally get what you worked for, you will really respect what's behind you. That's why when I see these young kids come straight up to the NHL without the benefit of any minor league experience, I think about the important early training they are missing.

I study these kids today, and I can see that they are bubbling over with talent, so much talent that it's hard to believe. On the other hand, they don't always take advantage of what they have. When practices are over, they're gone; they're the first ones off the ice when they could be doing more for themselves by staying out and improving their style.

Part of their problem is that they never had the benefit of minor league experience, and they don't really respect work. Times have changed.

"I considered myself luckier than most guys because I had been told I'd never play hockey again . . . . "

— *Doug Barkley*

7

Doug Barkley

Few professional athletes have experienced a more poign- antly tragic career than has Doug Barkley, coach of the Detroit Red Wings.

After laboring without notice for many years in the minors, Barkley finally was elevated to the National Hockey League as a full-time defenseman in 1962. The tall, hard- shooting western Canadian became an instant hit with the Detroit sextet. During the 1963-1964 season, he led the NHL defensemen in scoring (with 11 goals) and seemed destined for a long and successful big league career, when tragedy suddenly struck.

On the night of January 30, 1966, Doug Mohns, the Chicago Black Hawks left wing, accidentally struck Barkley with his stick. The blade of Mohn's stick creased Barkely's right eye. Despite intensive medical care Barkley lost the sight of the eye and was forced to retire as an active player just as he was reaching the peak of his career.

The Red Wings kept him on the payroll as an administrative assistant, and in 1969 he began another minor league career — as coach of the Fort Worth Wings, Detroit's farm club in the Central Professional League.

Once again, Doug Barkley had to plough through the minors to reach the NHL, but this time he didn't have to wait very long. Before the 1970-71 season was half over, Doug had been summoned to Detroit to become coach of the NHL Red Wings.

Barkley held court for this interview in his suite at the Warwick Hotel in Philadelphia. He had just concluded a meeting with veterans Gordie Howe and Gary Bergman.

Unlike some of the other subjects in this book Barkley appeared uneasy and distracted by the prospects of the impending game on that night of January 31, 1971, against the Philadelphia Flyers at the Spectrum. He wore a brown sports jacket, brown trousers, and tan desert boots.

After more than an hour of recalling his early hockey days, Doug excused himself to meet his players for a pre-game dinner. "Sometimes," he concluded, "I wish I had been discovered sooner in the minors. But that's the way life goes."

LETHBRIDGE, in the Alberta province of western Canada, was my home town. The town is rather unusual in terms of the weather. We have a wind there known as the "Chinook." On any given day the Chinook would come blowing through the mountain passes from the West Coast and warm everything in sight. The winter temperature used to be something like 5° below zero in the morning on my way to school, and I'd start thinking about playing hockey outdoors that afternoon. Then the Chinook would blow in while I was in school, and within four or five hours the thermometer would climb 50°, and all the ice would be melted by afternoon. When the Chinook disappeared, the temperature would dip as low as 40° below zero.

Lethbridge was a beautiful place to grow up. It's more than 3,000 feet above sea level and has more hours of sunshine than any other city in Canada, which is why they call it "The Land of the Big Sky." In the old days lots of coal was mined there on the banks of the Oldman River, but now the big industry is oil production.

My father was a yardman with the Canadian Pacific Railway in Lethbridge, and he worked for the CPR for 45 years. As far as hockey was concerned, my father always encouraged me. He always let me play in the basement of our house when it was too cold to play hockey outdoors — we'd use a tennis ball instead of a rubber puck. But I learned hockey mostly on the neighborhood rink.

My first pair of skates were hand-me-downs from my older brother when I was five years old. I started playing organized hockey when I was only six. As a matter of fact, you could say that I belonged to the New York Rangers organization when I was only six years old. It happened this way — the Rangers sponsored the Junior team in Lethbridge called the Native Sons. The Native Sons, in turn, had their own minor hockey program in the city, and the Peewee level team I played for was affiliated with the Native Sons. So at the age of six I was already playing in the Rangers' minor league chain.

At that time I played any position on the team that was offered to me, just as long as I could get ice. I played four years of Peewee hockey at a rink that was within walking distance of our home, which pleased my parents because it meant that I practiced my shooting against the rink's boards rather than against the side of the house.

Sometimes I'd play as many as four outdoor games in one day, playing for two teams in the school league and for a

Peewee and Bantam team in the regular organized league. Naturally, the trick was getting as much ice as possible. When I reached the age of ten I worked out an agreement with the icemaker at the outdoor rink so that I could clean the ice for him and in return get all the skating time I wanted. That was an excellent arrangement because as a "rink-rat," I got to meet a lot of the older Junior players, and they gave me a lot of their old skates that still were good enough for me to use. It wasn't until I was 14 that I got my first pair of new skates. My brother bought them for me.

Hockey wasn't the only sport on my mind. My father encouraged me to play all sports, and I became pretty good at basketball and football. When I got to high school, I had to make a decision that was to play a major part in my ultimate athletic career. The school had a ruling that if a student played hockey outside the school, he couldn't play football for them, so I had to make up my mind whether it was going to be football or hockey for Doug Barkley.

I decided on hockey because I liked it more than anything else. My heart was set on making it eventually to the New York Rangers because I had been connected with the Rangers' organization for so long. I remember wearing a jersey with a big Rangers crest on it. Once I had decided to forget football and basketball, I had to figure out just where I was going to move in hockey.

At the age of 16 it isn't always easy to make the proper decision, so I relied on the advice of Bob Lindsay, a teacher of mine in Lethbridge who had moved to the city of Medicine Hat. Lindsay suggested that it would be a good idea if I tried out for the Medicine Hat Junior team because the Lethbridge club was too strong, and there was no room for me in my home town.

I went to Medicine Hat without a pair of skates or anything to try out for the Junior club. When I got there, I borrowed a pair of skates from the team and worked out in three practices. It was then that they offered me a contract.

My coach was Alex Kaleta, who had played for the Chicago Black Hawks and New York Rangers in the NHL. That first coach in Juniors can have a very strong effect on a young player, and fortunately Kaleta was a good guy. He not only taught me hockey and gave me plenty of ice time — I really didn't know much about the game at all even though I had been playing for a long time — but he also boarded three of us at his home.

By then I had established that defense was my favorite position, and playing for Kaleta I managed to score 20 goals in that first year of Junior hockey on defense. Even if I hadn't scored that many goals I would have been happy. It was great to be 17 years old and playing in an organized league.

I considered myself luckier than most guys because I had been told I'd never play hockey again because of an accident I suffered while playing basketball. I had gone up for a shot, and when I came down a fellow fell right on my knee and snapped the cartilege right out. We managed to get it back in, but the thing used to snap back out all the time. That meant only one thing — surgery. I was in the hospital for only six days, and I was back working out in two weeks, wearing a brace on the knee and knowing that the doctor had said my playing career was over. That was something!

Kaleta was a big help all the time. He was a homebody type but also a disciplinarian and a great one for practicing. We'd come back from a loss on the road, and he would have us out practicing at 10 or 11 at night. Alex was strict, but for young players discipline is important.

We played against teams from Regina, Lethbridge, Moose Jaw, and Edmonton, and we traveled to road games by car. Thinking back on it, I always feel that the experience was unbelievable. That is, it is unbelievable that we survived traveling on the road to some of those games. It wasn't unusual to come up against snow in ten-foot drifts on the road with only one lane cleared for traffic in both directions. And there were big trucks going back and forth all the time. In some of those blizzards we never really knew what was coming at us, but we never had a real accident, although snow forced the cancellation of a few games. We never failed to show up for a game. Not one.

Most of the other teams in the league had their own buses, but we didn't have that kind of money, so we traveled by car. The players, who were 16, 17, and 18 years old, did the driving, but we didn't mind it. At that age a guy really likes to drive. It's different when you get older, though; the guys in their twenties didn't want to drive after a tough game.

From the start I had a pretty good shot for a defenseman, and I wound up second on the team in scoring in my first year of Junior hockey. Then the Chicago Black Hawks drafted me and invited me to their training camp in St. Catharines, Ontario. It was quite a kick for a kid my age because it was only the second time in my life that I had traveled East. I was with five other fellows from the West, and we took a train to Toronto and headed straight for St. Catharines, which was right nearby. Camp itself was quite an experience. I got lots of ice time, and I was only 17 years old and playing with all the big names from the NHL.

Since I only had one year of Junior hockey behind me, I really couldn't expect to make the NHL. I was satisfied to be assigned to the Calgary Stampeders of the Western League, which was a fast minor pro league. To tell the truth, I was quite surprised to jump up to the pros so fast because I was only 17, and I still had a lot to learn.

When I got to Calgary I was told I wasn't going to play very much because the club had veterans such as Freddie Hucul and Art Mitchell. However, some of the guys had injuries early in the season, so I got to play a regular shift almost immediately.

It was then, in that 1956-1957 season, that my career

almost ended. We were playing against the Saskatoon Quakers in Saskatoon, and I was standing in front of the Quakers' net, bracing myself for a pass, when one of the guys on the other team came along — I never saw him until it was too late — and crashed into me, hitting the outside of my good knee.

As soon as I went down I knew I was in big trouble. I was in great pain, and I couldn't skate. I was taken to the hospital and told that I'd be out of action for a year and would have to have surgery on the knee. At first the club doubted how serious it was and tried to get my knee back in shape with three weeks of therapy so I could be ready for the playoffs. But that didn't work, and I eventually had the operation.

This time I really believed my career over. I wasn't even 20 yet, and I had had operations on both knees and would have to wear a brace on each one when I played. It was hardly a promising way to try to make the NHL.

To strengthen my legs I went to a health studio in Calgary and worked out with weights on my knees; that seemed to help. When I reported to the Black Hawks camp in St. Catharines that fall, I thought I might have a chance to stay with the big team. But that was the year that defenseman Pierre Pilote and Elmer Vasko made the club, and the Hawks also added Al Arbour from Detroit, Jack Evans from New York, and Dollard St. Laurent from Montreal. So instead of being third defenseman, as I originally hoped I would, I wound up as sixth defenseman and out of a job! So they sent me back to Calgary, and I continued the minor league grind in the Western League.

Playing in the Western League had its advantages. There were teams in Vancouver, Seattle, and Spokane at the time, so we did quite a bit of flying instead of traveling by bus the way they do in the American League. After a while the league added teams in San Francisco, Los Angeles, and Portland, which made traveling very interesting.

The pay wasn't too good; in fact, meal money was very

low — about $4.50 to $5 a day. But when we traveled by train we just signed for the meals and the tab was picked up by the team. Train travel really was the best because we could move all around the cars, play cards, and relax a lot more than we could on the bus.

Once I had become a part of the Black Hawks farm system, the front office alternated me between Calgary and the other farm team in Buffalo. As a result I had quite a variety of coaches. In Calgary I had Frank Currie, who was not very tough, and in Buffalo I had the late Frankie Eddolls, who was also a soft type. I also had Gus Kýle and Alfie Pike in Calgary and they were really tough on the guys.

My first season in Buffalo was 1957-1958. We seemed to be on the bus all the time, traveling to places like Quebec City, Hershey, and Baltimore. We saw a lot of accidents in those buses, and we came close to having many ourselves. At the first of the year, the team usually would get a regular bus driver who had been driving for years and knew the roads really well. He was a good driver, and we didn't have to worry for the rest of the season. But a lot of the driving was through winter storms, and there were times that it took us eight or nine hours to reach a rink that should have been only two or three hours away.

Year after year in the minors I kept hoping that I'd be noticed and called up to the NHL to stay, but it didn't happen. In the 1960-1961 season I scored 9 goals and 28 assists for 37 points and I thought, "Well, this might be my break; maybe they'll call me up." But nothing happened.

I can't complain about the teams, though. We had some good clubs in Buffalo, with solid players like Bill Sweeney, Parker MacDonald, Bruce Cline, and Marcel Paille. There were triumphs, and there were tragedies. One of the tragedies happened to Bill Dobbyn, a fine young defenseman with our Buffalo club.

Bill was playing in a game at Hershey one night, when he was hit in the eye with a stick and lost his sight. That accident ended the career of a guy who almost certainly would have made it to the NHL.

One of the weird things about playing for Buffalo was that the club was run by both the New York Rangers and the Chicago Black Hawks. This meant there were so many good players on the team that many of us often wound up on the bench not playing at all. They'd play a man for a while and then sit him out because some player had just been shipped down from New York or Chicago to be tried out.

During my last year at Buffalo, Orland Kurtenbach, who went on to become a star at Vancouver, and I balanced out the bench. We both weighed about the same and were about the same height. So he sat at one end of the bench and I sat at the other. As a result of not playing so much and from balancing the bench, the two of us wound up becoming good friends.

By then I began wondering just what it was that kept me from getting a chance in the NHL. I later was told by some people in the Detroit Red Wings organization, including Sid Abel and Jimmy Skinner, that scouts felt that I didn't have enough stamina to make it in the majors. They felt that I couldn't last in the fastest league.

I assume they made that judgment based on the fact that I wasn't in the best of condition when I played for Buffalo. The reason for that, of course, was that I didn't get enough ice time. When I did go out there I'd get tired quickly because I played so little.

The first big turning point in my attempts to become a major leaguer occured in the fall of 1961. Instead of being sent back to Buffalo, the Black Hawks shipped me to Calgary, which really made me happy because Calgary was close to my home and friends. I said to myself, "Well, I'm

going to play for the Stampeders and do the best job I can."
In fact, I began to think about settling permanently in
Calgary, forgetting about the NHL, getting an off-season job
with an oil company, and becoming a part of the community.

Right after I made that decision things really started
coming my way. For starters, Alfie Pike was my coach, and
he gave me all the confidence I needed as a player; this is of
tremendous importance. He played me between 50 and 55
minutes of a 60-minute game and just let me go out there on
the ice.

Lots of people wonder how a man can play 55 minutes in
modern hockey with all the speed and pressure. What I did
was alternate my style. For a few minutes I'd move the puck,
then I'd switch to a passing game. Or I'd get a breather just
by playing the point on the power play. Other things that
helped, believe it or not, were penalties and fights, which
allowed me time to go over to the boards and rest.

Besides, I was only 25 years old at the time, and I had a lot
of stamina. And, like Gordie Howe when he was in his
heyday with the Red Wings, I learned to rest while actually
playing on the ice. I just had to pick my spots. I'd go all out
if I was killing a penalty, and then I'd come off for a minute's
rest.

My knees were no longer a problem. I had worried about
them at first and wore the braces. Then I figured I ought to
find out just how strong the legs were, so I took off the
braces and just played with a little elastic brace over my
knees. I never had any problems after that. Nothing bothered
me in that 1961-1962 season in Calgary. I played in 70 games
and scored 25 goals and 49 assists for 74 points. I set two
Western League records.

That was a season in which I can still remember specific
games. One night in Spokane I got three goals and two assists
— my biggest point-getting night ever — against Eddie

Johnston, the goalie who later went up to the Boston Bruins.

That same year I played in the league All-Star game in Portland and was voted the most valuable player in the game. Looking back I have to laugh because in those days they didn't give out big trophies — just little replicas of the bigger awards. But after I won the MVP award in the All-Star game, they gave me a trophy that was three feet high. When the team headed back from Portland to Calgary I got stopped by a Customs officer when he saw the gigantic trophy. He asked me how much it was worth, and I told him I didn't know, that he should figure out what it was worth. The guy finally let me through without any more hassle.

It wouldn't be fair for me to take all the credit for my improvement that season: I had some really fine teammates, especially Sandy Hucul and George McAvoy on defense. All this time I was hoping that some NHL scouts were watching me. When you have a good year, you're always hoping you're being scouted.

In those days scouting wasn't the way it is now. Then if there was one scout at a game that was really something; now there are probably eight or ten scouts at every game. Before the players used to worry more about the game in front of them than about the scouts in the stands.

At the end of the 1961-1962 season, I returned to Calgary and drove a cement mixer to stay in shape. Shifting those gears really helped build up my wrists and arms, and it didn't hurt my knees either. But my future was still a big question mark.

Then it happened.

One afternoon in June I heard on the radio that Chicago had traded me to Detroit for Len Lunde and John McKenzie, a pair of forwards. I was very, very pleased. Next I got a letter from Sid Abel, the Red Wings' coach, inviting me to training camp.

As soon as that happened, I checked into the health studio

and worked extra hard with the weights so that I would be in top shape when training camp opened. That was my chance for a shot at the NHL, and I wasn't going to miss it if I could help it.

Even at the age of 25, I wasn't too old to get excited as I headed for the Red Wings' training camp in Detroit. I was pleased even more when I got to Detroit. It was a really great camp, and the management told me that they needed me and really planned to use me. Of course I still had to make the club, but if I did make it, I wasn't going to be riding the bench as a fifth or sixth defenseman.

When I think back on it all, I often wonder about the crazy turns life takes. I had been with the Chicago organization for eight years, and the year before I had been traded to Detroit I hadn't even been invited to the Black Hawks' training camp. The possibilities of playing in the NHL were never more remote then, but a year later I was in the camp with Gordie Howe, Alex Delvecchio, and Marcel Pronovost. I was really overjoyed.

I had changed quite a bit from my early days in Calgary. When I turned pro I weighed 185 pounds and was 6'2½". When I showed up at the Red Wings' camp I weighed 195.

On my first day in camp I discovered that the rest of the players were going to play golf. One of them asked me if I wanted to go along.

I said "Geez, I'd like to, but I don't have any clubs or shoes or anything."

A day or so earlier Gordie Howe had hurt his hand and had to rest. He was there at the golf arena at the time, and when he heard what I had said, he came over to me.

"What size shoe do you wear?" Howe asked.

I said, "Oh, ten, ten-and-a-half."

He said, "You can use mine. Here they are, take them."

Gordie made me feel at home right at the beginning of camp, and it was really great for me with the Red Wings from that point on.

The other man who helped was Sid Abel, the coach of Detroit. He was easy to talk to, and he let me play a lot. There were times when I was playing when I was dead tired, but Sid would say, "Okay, Alex, Gordie, Gadsby, and Doug get on the ice." And I'd go out because I figured if Gordie could make it, I could make it.

I did make it with the Red Wings that year. I played 70 games and scored 3 goals and 24 assists for 27 points. I really felt that I belonged. I stayed in the NHL until just past the middle of the 1965-1966 season, when I got hit in the eye with Doug Mohns' stick during a game against Chicago. I never recovered full sight in the eye, and I had to retire as a player.

I became a scout for the Red Wings and ended up in the minors again. I was able to go into all the buildings and see the different coaching techniques at work. I knew most of the coaches or general managers, and I sat around and talked with them and listened to their problems. Guys in hockey are good about talking with each other all the time. That way a newcomer can learn a lot about handling men and handling the game.

Eventualiy, I became a coach in the Red Wings' minor league system in 1969, running the Fort Worth Wings, the Detroit club's top farm team in the Central Hockey League. When that happened, I tried to piece together all the information I had learned from coaching in the minor leagues and to apply it to my young players in Fort Worth.

I demanded 100 percent effort. My system was basic — hard checking and playing the body. I liked tough defensemen, and I figured that with tough defensemen and fast skating, good forechecking forwards, I could mold a good team.

I felt that I should treat each player differently because each has his own personality. Some players can be pushed, while others don't need any pushing. Some skaters will quit on you if you push too hard. After a while, I learned that if the team wasn't giving 100 percent effort, some experimentation was necessary. In some cases it was necessary first to jump on a guy to get some response. If that didn't work, another angle had to be explored. And if that didn't work, there was no use having the player on the team.

It didn't take very long before I had an opportunity to put my minor league coaching experience to practice in the majors. On January 10th, 1971, I was named the coach of the Detroit Red Wings.

"If you want something bad enough, you can do it."

— *Reggie Fleming*

8

Reggie Fleming

Reggie Fleming is stocky and solid, with the "bull" neck you expect of a "policeman," which is what he has been throughout his career. Reggie has played for three minor league teams since he turned pro in 1956-1957, and he has also policed the National Hockey League for Chicago, New York, Philadelphia, and Buffalo. He is usually a center or left wing, but he has also been known to play defense.

When we first met Reggie as a New York Ranger, he had the close crewcut of an athlete, but when we sat down to almost two hours of taping at New York's Statler Hilton Hotel, his hair was long, and his clothes verged on being "mod." Reggie's is the classic case of Teddy Roosevelt's motto, "Talk softly and carry a big stick," for he is indeed tough on the ice, but he has a soft voice in private. He is an old-fashioned cigarette-lighting, door-opening gentleman, as are many hockey players. It was the day before a Buffalo-New York game, and when we met Reggie for breakfast at 10 A.M., he had been up for hours.

Reggie has a home in Chicago and has become an alien resident of the United States. He is married to an American ex-stewardess, and he loves to play golf and spend time with his family when he isn't involved with hockey. Reggie has an off-season job working with food warehouses. He hopes to retire to that lovely home in Chicago one day, but he just might coach in the minors if the chance develops.

LIKE those of many other youngsters from Montreal, some of my first memories as a child are of skating and playing hockey. I guess I was about four or five years old when I began skating. I lived with my grandmother in the eastern part of the city near Delormier Downs (race track) in a nice house with a garden. I have an uncle who is only 19 days older than I, and the two of us used to water down the garden with a hose and skate there. Sometimes we'd skate at the city park about two or three blocks away from our house. We would put on our skates at home, and because the roads were usually icy, we'd skate our way to the park.

And sometimes we'd play hockey in the streets, using a couple of cans as goalposts. So even when I was very young, I was always on skates. I never played real team hockey, though, until I went to school at St. Dominic's, when I was seven or eight years old. When I was in the 7th grade, I was fortunate because I got to play class hockey and church hockey, which included fellows up to 17 and 18 years old.

The church league was an organized league, consisting of kids from St. Dominic's church school as well as kids from outside the school who lived in the parish of St. Dominic's. I lived outside the parish, but I attended the school, so I got to play in the church league. Some of the Brothers who taught at the school used to play with us. So I sometimes played with or against the principal and teachers. Anytime I was mad at one of them, I could take it out on the ice!

I was a centerman from the very beginning. I loved to carry the puck and to forecheck. I felt the centerman was the one who controlled the game, just like the quarterback in football.

St. Dominic's was mainly an English school, although I lived in a predominantly French neighborhood. I started school in a French school, but my parents switched me to St. Dominic's.

The English kids and the French kids got along pretty well in my neighborhood when I was a kid. Oh sure, we called them "pea-soupers" and they called us "blokes" and stuff like that. And we used to have some scrapes, too. But they were mostly just kids' fights, not real gang activity.

By the time I was 12 years old, I was playing hockey just about every day — in class hockey, church hockey, and Midget hockey. The next year we moved to an English neighborhood so that I could attend D'Arcy McGee high school in Montreal, and I began to play interscholastic hockey and Midget hockey with a Park Extension district team. The Park Extension Midget hockey was affiliated with the Montreal Canadiens' organization, so at the age of 13, I was already a part of the National League system. My interscholastic league included several high schools besides my own: Loyola, Catholic High, Westhill, and Westmount. This league was better scouted than the Midget hockey league because we played most of our games in the Forum.

I really loved outdoor hockey. It was tough because we never knew what the weather was going to be like, and sometimes games were canceled because of bad weather. But it was great because of the way we worked together. If there was snow, we'd find a plow and clean the ice together. There was that kind of togetherness between teams as well as among teammates.

I found that I forgot the weather in the fun of playing. It

was 15° below zero, but nobody worried about it. Hockey players don't really freeze because they're too active.

As far as I can recall, none of the kids I played class hockey and church hockey with ever went to pro leagues. The only kids I ever knew in school who went into professional sports played football. I played football in high school, and one fellow I played with is now on the Ottawa team, and another is playing pro ball in Montreal.

One reason I chose hockey over football was because of my Dad. He had played pro football and had been the trainer for the Montreal Alouettes. He told me to stay away from football because there's no money in Canadian football — at least not for Canadians. They draft American imports, and the American imports make all the big money in Canadian football.

My dad soured me on football, but I don't recall that he pushed me toward hockey. My parents didn't mind that I played the game, and they bought my skates. And Dad had some contacts at the Forum who gave me all the sticks I needed.

I remember that my grandmother and her sister, who were both from Poland, used to say to me, "You're playing hockey, but what about your schooling? You've got to go to school, go to school, go to school!" And my mother would turn around to them and say, "Look, if he wants to play hockey, let him play hockey. He's my son." I will always remember how my mother stuck up for me.

As it turned out, I did finish high school, but I never graduated. I was very lucky because I got an extra year of school when I went to Toronto and attended St. Michael's. It was a little like having a year of college. I never graduated from there either because I became ill. But I still got more education than a lot of hockey players did then.

As I look back on the coaches and training I received during those early years, I remember one childhood coach in particular. At St. Dominic's there was a fifth grade teacher named Emmett Mulholland, a fantastic fellow. He was a bachelor, and he spent all of his free time coaching for an orphanage as well as for a team at a French school in his district. I got to know him when I had a class with him. At St. Dominic's we used to pick our best players to form a team to play against this French team he coached. Well, his team was so organized that they whipped us to death. And we had some good hockey players! But Mulholland had taught them a system that could beat us. After that whipping, Mulholland asked me to practice with his team, and I learned his system.

Young kids — especially today — don't know how to pass a puck or how to shoot. And in hockey all the kids want to handle the puck; nobody wants to hand it off. In those practices with Mulholland, I learned for the first time that you can't be an individual in hockey. I learned how to pass the puck, how to headman the puck, and how to get in position to get it back. With his team it was all positional play and teamwork. I guess I must have worked out with his club for more than a year, and then he was killed in an auto crash; it was a terrible loss and the end of a valuable experience for me.

Another great period in my life was in high school in the interscholastic league. My Midget league was good and almost won a city championship one year, but the interscholastic league was better for me personally because of my coach, Brother Paul, and because we played and practiced at the Forum.

We had Saturday morning practices at the Forum, and D'Arcy McGee had its own locker there. So I would get the locker key from Brother Paul and go there all alone at 6:30 on Saturday mornings, an hour and a half before our practices. Skating all by myself around that place was just like a New York City kid going to Yankee Stadium and throwing the ball by himself from the pitcher's mound. The Forum was *the end* for me, the place where the best played. I'd get the puck at one end and make a rush with my head down, all the way to the other end. I'd score a goal and raise my hands, and I thought that was the greatest.

Dickie Moore became my idol when I started high school because he had gone to D'Arcy McGee for a year and had played in Park Extension. So I tried to model myself after him. He was aggressive, a team leader, and just a fantastic man. Later when I heard how he had struggled with his bad knees, I admired him even more.

When I was playing at that age, I was really lucky in that I got a lot of good ice time. I'd kill penalties, execute the power play, and take a regular shift on a line. A player does his best when he gets all that action. I was lucky enough to make the interscholastic All-Star team the couple of years I played.

One year we were playing Catholic High, which was noted for its great hockey. They had a lot of really good French players. One of them stole the puck from me during a game, and he made me look like a fool. Boy, did I get mad. He took the puck back into his own zone and started winding up. He came out to center ice, and as he cut from the boards in the center, I was coming from the opposite wing. Well, I caught him with a really good, hard legal check; I put him out — completely knocked him out! And from there we went on to win our game. The referee of the game was also a reporter for the high school interscholastic games, and after the game he came up to me and said, "In all my years, that's the hardest check I ever saw anyone put out or receive." And that just stuck in my mind; if you want something enough, you can do it — and I had wanted that puck back!

The other event that stands out from my interscholastic days is the time that the D'Arcy McGee team got to go to Toronto to play a junior team there, the Toronto Marlboros

Junior B club. Carl Brewer and Al MacNeil and a lot of really good players were on that club. They really trounced us, 11-2, but we had one heck of a good fight in that game. One of the players got into a fight and the next thing we knew, the whole team jumped in. We had a Chinese goaltender, a good guy named Normie Wong, and even he came out and joined the fight. I ended up getting thrown out of the game, and there were only five or six minutes left to play anyway. We had a good bunch of fellows on that team, and we stuck together.

Outside the interscholastic league I played only one year of Midget hockey, and then I went on to Junior B with a club called Hochelaga (the Indian word for Montreal). The Metropolitan League in Montreal was a kind of confusing situation. The Montreal Royals Senior hockey team sponsored Montreal Royals Junior A and Junior B clubs. The Montreal Canadiens sponsored a Montreal Canadiens Junior A club, a Junior B club, and the Hochelaga Junior B club. And the Junior B was completely different from Midget because, instead of consisting of kids from only one district, the Junior B players were recruited from all over the city.

From the first day I played organized, sponsored hockey, I played pro rules. The only real differences were that in interscholastic hockey if we fought, we were suspended for a game, which could really hurt the club. So we curtailed our fighting. And in the Midget League, although the games were 60 minutes as in the pro games, the clock wasn't stopped with the action stopped, so it was a running game and therefore shorter than pro games. And the schedule was shorter; in the Midget League it had been maybe 16 games; in Junior B it jumped to about 34 games; and in Junior A we were playing a 48-game schedule.

I played Junior B hockey with the Hochelaga club for one year, and I was still getting good ice time. Then I got a letter from Sam Pollock inviting me to try out with the Junior A

Canadiens camp the next fall. I knew that I had been scouted within the Midget and Junior B leagues, but I think he knew of me mainly because of my interscholastic hockey — because we played at the Forum.

I made the Junior A team that fall, but as the fourth centerman on the team, I didn't see much action. They had Henri Richard, Phil Goyette, and Ron Atwell that year, so I was really behind. If we were ahead by a big score, I got to play the last few minutes. It's a funny thing about coaches in Junior hockey. They don't worry as much about the development of players as they do about that score. They didn't have to worry about how Phil and Henri developed, but a fellow like me, who didn't have as much basic talent as those two, needed the work and the development. But I only got to fill in.

Had I stayed in Junior B for another year, I probably would have gotten more ice time and more attention, but because of my age, I could only qualify for Junior A for three years. I would have missed a year of Junior A if I had stayed behind. As it was, I got two years with the Junior A Canadiens and a year at St. Michael's, and even though I didn't play much, I got some valuable experience.

There were an awful lot of good players and great teams in Junior hockey at that time. I mentioned Phil and Henri, but we also had Claude Provost. Although we only played in Quebec my first year of Junior A, the second year we played a lot in Ontario. And that league had the Toronto Marlboros, Toronto St. Mike's, Guelph, Galt, Barrie, Kitchener, and even St. Catharine's. There were greats like Frank Mahovlich, Carl Brewer, Al MacNeil, Bobbie Baun, Billy Harris, Eddie Shack, Moose Vasko, and Bobby Hull. The league was loaded with talent. By my second year of Junior A I was switched back to defense, and I began to get a little more ice time. Elmer Lach was coaching, and he switched me. Even though I had been switched to defense and saw a little more action, I still didn't take a regular turn and never did in Montreal. Then for my third year of Junior A, I went to Toronto.

That next year the Montreal Junior Canadiens decided to withdraw from a regular league schedule and go on tour. I believe they ended up playing something like 103 games that year! They went from eastern Canada to western Canada playing exhibition games — and they had great drawing power. I wanted to stay in school but I couldn't if I stayed with the Junior Canadiens on tour. So, although I was still the property of the Canadiens, I went on loan to Toronto St. Michael's. I think it was easy for Mr. Pollock to let me do this, because I don't think I was really a part of his plans anyway. The Canadiens had always been skaters, passers, and puckhandlers, and I wasn't noted for my skating ability or my finesse. The only way I have ever made it was by working hard and running into people. So off I went to Toronto, where I got more valuable ice time.

There were great fans of Junior hockey in Toronto. We used to play in Maple Leaf Gardens on Sunday afternoons, and it would be absolutely packed. They would have doubleheaders on Sundays, and the better team would be scheduled second, to be sure that the crowd would stay.

The next fall ended my Junior career. I then got my first invitation to the Canadiens' camp. After about a week at camp, they started shunting players around. They had to supply players to the Montreal Royals and to their team in Shawinigan Falls, Quebec. I went to Shawinigan Falls.

It was great in some ways but in others it was tough. The general manager at that time was Kenny Reardon, and the coach was Roger Leger, a former Canadiens great. Things really change in the pros. Suddenly you're a pro and hockey is your bread and butter, not just a fun game you like to play. In Junior hockey I could still go to school, but in the pros I had to make a decision: was I going to be a pro, or was I going to try to continue my education? Well, my education was nil, as far as degrees went, and I was left with trying to make it as a pro in strange surroundings. I knew I wasn't going to jump right up to the NHL right then — there was just too much talent around.

So I began my first year of professional hockey as a fifth or sixth defenseman in Shawinigan Falls. As a matter of fact, at one point early in the season they were going to reinstate me as an amateur and ship me down to Kingston, in the Ontario Senior League. Then a defenseman got hurt in practice, so they kept me in Shawinigan.

About a month after the season started, Kenny Reardon had a little talk with me. He said to me, "You know, Fleming, I could sign you to a $10,000 contract for practices (I had signed a standard $3,500 contract plus a $500 signing bonus for turning pro). That's how much you're worth in practice. But you're not worth a damn in a game!"

Well, that's the way I was — I worked hard in practices all the time, while some of the other guys never took practice seriously. But in a game, where it meant winning or losing, I used to get terribly nervous. I didn't want to make mistakes. So I worried, and there were times when I didn't play such a hot game; but I also think my performance suffered because of lack of experience and lack of confidence in the coach.

I didn't have such a great year, but we had a pretty good bunch of fellows. We had George Faulkner, who was a good minor leaguer for years; Claude LaForge, who played with Detroit and Philadelphia; and Andre Pronovost and "Junior" Langlois, both with the Canadiens later.

The following year we had a new coach, Fred Shero. He took basically the same team, made a couple of changes, and we ended up in second place and went on to win the championship. There were four teams in the Quebec Senior League: Quebec, Three Rivers, Shawinigan, and the Montreal Royals. We played Montreal first and won 4 out of 7; then we did the same to Quebec.

I really appreciated Fred. I was single and I boarded. I was never much of a sleeper; I used to get up early nearly every morning and walk the streets. Then I'd go to a restaurant and have my breakfast and Fred, also an early riser, would be there. After breakfast we'd go to the rink. Fred would put on his skates, too, and we'd go out on the ice and really work out. He gave me many pointers on those mornings. He taught me how to stride a little better. He pointed out to me that the style of hockey skating is less like figure skating and more like speed skating, that if you want to skate well, you have to figure out how speed skaters turn and stride and crouch. He taught me how to strengthen my wrists and how to hold a stick. When you hold a stick, you should always have both hands on it, or you will get tired right away. And he'd say to me, "How many good guys are remembered? How many good guys make the team? Never worry about people talking about you, whether it's good or bad. They know you're there; it's when they stop talking about you that you have to start worrying."

Shawinigan Falls is a pulp and paper town of about 20,000 people, and it's all French. The people knew me there, and they knew that when I went out on the ice, I gave 100 percent. Shawinigan is where I became known as a fighter, and people seem to love fights. And Fred Shero sort of egged me on to be more aggressive. He'd say, "Don't you worry about the fines. You just go out there and do your best, and if you have to fight, then fight!"

I got so close to Fred that he gave me permission to go to Montreal on Saturday nights to watch the Canadiens games at the Forum with my father, who had season tickets. We were usually scheduled to play in Montreal on Sundays so I'd just drive up there the night before. And one time I invited Fred to a Canadiens game with me. We went to the game and sat behind the bench and he pointed lots of things out to me.

We went to a game together the night the Canadiens

played the Chicago Black Hawks. Chicago's great goalie was Glenn Hall. Fred knew Glenn because he had attended hockey clinics with him. After the game Fred introduced me to Hall and he said to Hall, "You know, one day this kid is going to be in the NHL. And he's going to be on the same club you are, and he's going to help you out."

What he said seemed strange to me because I was Montreal property, and it looked as though I would be forever. Besides, from what anybody could tell at that point, I might never make it to the NHL at all! But it ultimately turned out that Fred was right on the button, and I'll never forget it!

What built up my confidence in Shawinigan most was Fred. I had heard that Reardon didn't want me played, but Shero played me on both forward and defense, wherever he could use me. I felt that he was a guy who really wanted to help me, and I did my best for him. And it finally paid off for both of us.

We were in the finals of the playoffs against Quebec. I didn't get to play in several of those games, so I would sit in the press box in the stands and watch the team. I would get so excited watching that I was always yelling, "Hit 'em! Hit 'em!"

After one such game, Phil Watson, the New York Rangers' coach at the time, who had been listening to me yell encouragement to the team, said to me, "You know, Fleming, you'll never make the NHL because all you ever think of is hitting."

"Well, Phil," I said, "all I know is that the only man I ever heard of who could score from the seat of his pants was Rocket Richard. It's pretty hard to score when you're on your back!"

During the last game against Quebec, my spirits started to rise. We had a 35-goal scorer, a little redheaded guy named Danny Ray. Danny was having a good playoff — and I was getting down in the dumps because I wasn't being used. Then in the practice before the last game I suddenly thought, "What if Fred decides to use me and I'm not in shape? Then I'll not only blame myself, but the team will, too." So I worked really hard in that practice; I stayed an extra half hour, did some stops and starts, got a sweat jacket, and really worked.

Sure enough, Fred benched Ray and used me. I asked Fred later what made him change his mind, and he told me that this scorer had too many goals against him when he was on the ice, so he decided to use an aggressive guy who would work both ways. And that was me. Our line scored three goals that night, and I got a goal and a couple of assists. A linemate got the winning goal from my assist, and we won the championship in overtime, 4-3. I really felt great, and Fred's confidence in me had paid off.

Traveling in the Quebec Senior League was tough, especially when we went to Chicoutimi. It wasn't just the distance but the *weather* — we never knew what to expect. There was a huge hunting and fishing reserve on the way to Chicoutimi, and when the weather was really bad, they'd close the park and we'd have to detour. Sometimes the bus would break down and we'd sit in cold you wouldn't believe. And we were always living on sandwiches and milk or pop, never a hot meal. We'd leave right after a game, eat cold sandwiches on the road, and get in from Chicoutimi at three in the morning. Then we'd have practice at nine the next morning or a game the next night. And there weren't any of the fringe benefits that there are today. We never even knew which of us would be playing because there were always at least two or three extra players.

One good thing was that there weren't the pressures in the minor leagues that there are in the NHL, but that was because there wasn't as much money or fame involved. The year we won the championship we earned only an $800 bonus, and there was little real prestige in winning that championship. The series was also very prolonged because they didn't want to compete with NHL attendance. We'd play Wednesdays and Sundays, instead of playing three or four games a week to get the series over with.

My life in Shawinigan Falls was very simple. I paid my landlady $15 a week and two hockey tickets and she would clean my room and do my laundry. For meals I went downstairs to another woman, and she charged me maybe $1 or $1.50 a meal.

Living in a town where everyone knew us had its disadvantages. It meant a certain amount of hero worship, but it also meant that everyone knew our business. We couldn't go for just one beer, because townspeople would say we had had ten! We shopped at the same stores all the time, and after we saw the local movie, it was there for the rest of the week. So we'd go to the local pool hall and shoot a little pool or maybe play some cards and have a couple beers in the local saloon. But there was little time or opportunity to date, and we always had to watch ourselves.

One form of entertainment was to go 15 miles to watch the boxing matches on cable television on Wednesday nights off. Fred was a boxing enthusiast, and he had once been a good boxer. He would take three or four of us in his car to Grand Maire since they didn't have cable television in Shawinigan. As a matter of fact I seldom watched television at all in Shawinigan since it was the landlord's set and the programs were strictly in French.

The scene with my landlords was kind of funny. They spoke English with me sometimes, and I spoke French with them quite often. They were very nice to me, but after a while I discovered that they didn't think I was Canadian because I wasn't French. To them, if you weren't French, you couldn't be Canadian!

But after two years at Shawinigan Falls, I was promoted to Rochester, New York, in the American League. That year in

Rochester was kind of strange. For one thing, we had three coaches in one season. We started off with Bucko McDonald. After he left, Sam Pollock coached a couple of games, and finally the coaching went to former defenseman Steve Kraftcheck. The other funny thing was that out of about 16 players, 9 of us were rookies. This wasn't a stable club because at that time both Toronto and Montreal were sponsoring Rochester, and a lot of young guys were being shuttled up and down.

Even with the confusion we had a pretty good club that year. Billy Hicke turned pro that season, won the rookie award, and scored something like 94 points. We had veteran center Rudy Migay, down from Toronto; Al MacNeil on defense with me; and Gary Aldcorn, a wing who was going up and down between Toronto and Rochester. MacNeil, Aldcorn, Migay, and I rented a huge home together for the season, and later we were joined by Bob Nevin, who traveled back and forth between Rochester and Chicoutimi. The league was full of guys who later went on to the NHL and guys who were on their last legs, coming down from the NHL.

In the American League there is better competition and better players than in the Quebec Senior League. It was the top of the minors. People use to put it in terms of percentage: the NHL was the 100 percent bracket of performance; the AHL was the 65-75 percent bracket; and it went down 10 percent through the Western and Central Leagues, and so on.

By this time I guess I was up to making $4,000 a year, which seemed like good money. Every player signs a "C" form when they first affiliate with a parent NHL organization. Over the years, as we sign with higher status clubs, we receive a signing fee, which totals $1,000 by the time you sign into the NHL. So I had received $500 for signing with the Quebec Senior League and I got another $250 when I went into the AHL. I must have received the final $250 when

I signed with Chicago later. I don't even know if youngsters have to sign this form anymore. It's a kind of a "con" deal, but when you're a young kid who just loves to play the game, the fact that they pay you to do what you love is a big thing.

We had a tougher schedule in the AHL than I had ever played before. We used to play three games in three nights – Friday, Saturday, and Sunday. We'd play at home on Friday night, grab the bus to Cleveland for Saturday night, and then turn right around and run back to Rochester for Sunday night.

We'd sleep on the bus, eat on the bus — everything. But we had some good trips. The togetherness is much more obvious on a bus trip than it is on a plane. First of all, the trip usually lasts four or five hours rather than the hour and a half a plane might take. And you could walk around more comfortably on a bus. We had a lot of card players, so we'd play poker, read a lot, and sing.

Of course, by this time I was doing a lot of hitting because hitting is my bread and butter. I have to compensate for the finesse that a Mikita or an Esposito has by playing the other guy's body, by taking him out of the play. Take a skater like John McKenzie who is smooth and fast. If we had a race into the corner to get the puck, Johnny would win. But if he knows I'm coming in behind him and that I'm not going to play the puck but hit the man, he's going to lose a stride or two, hesitating. And then this gives me a 50-50 chance of getting to the puck first.

Actually I can't remember any colossal fights that I was in myself, but I do remember a brawl someone else was in. I played that season with Murray Balfour, who was my size, about 5'8" and 175 pounds. And there was another guy in the league, Bob Bailey, who had a reputation as a really bad guy. He was really supposed to be tough, and big — maybe 210 pounds. Well, during this one game, little Murray took on Bailey and really pounded him. And this went on all season; every time they played against each other, Murray would give Bailey a terrible pounding.

The following year I began the season with Rochester and played my first 15 games there. Then Toronto took over the Rochester club entirely, and I was demoted to Kingston. This was really confusing because Boston owned Kingston, but Boston had a player loan deal with Montreal at the time. There was a player named Picard playing for Ottawa-Hull, owned by Boston, and Montreal wanted him, so I was sent to Kingston. Well, I refused to go — I didn't want to play in Kingston. Montreal owned two clubs in the league, and I couldn't understand why I couldn't be on one of their clubs. Management told me to take my complaint to Sam Pollock, so I called him. There was going to be a game in Kingston that night, Saturday, so Sam asked me to play just that one game with Kingston and then to come to see him in Ottawa the next day. Being the naive kid I was, I did what he told me, and although we lost the game, I had a great night on defense, getting four assists. And the next day I saw Sam Pollock in Ottawa. Good, old "fast-talking" Sam persuaded me to stick it out with Kingston and definitely gave me the idea that I was their number one defenseman in the minors. I walked away with the distinct impression that the next injury in Montreal meant that I was going to be called up. Well, I went back to Kingston and sure enough, one of the Canadiens got hurt and guess who was called up — J. C. Tremblay! He was having a great season in Ottawa-Hull that year, and there went my dreams.

Meanwhile, although I ended up having a pretty good year in Kingston, with 19 goals and 49 assists, I was miserable. First of all, the team had a lot of men who had come down and were on their last legs. They liked their beer and their fooling around too much for a "gung-ho" kid like me, and I wasn't very impressed with them. Nor was I very impressed with management — there were too many chiefs to suit me.

Cal Gardner was our coach and I liked him, but Cal was between the chiefs and the goof-offs, and his hands were pretty well tied.

Once when we were playing the Montreal Royals (by this time it's no longer the Quebec Senior League but the Pro League) they had a really tough guy named Wally Clune. When he had a chance to body check, he'd really bash a guy. During play the puck had been deflected right up in the air, and one of our guys was just standing there looking up for the puck. I could see Clune barreling along, so I yelled, "Look out!" Well, the puck came down and Clune didn't hit the guy — just missed him. But our player had lost possession of the puck. So when he came off the ice after the whistle blew, he started cursing, "Who in the hell was yelling at me?" And I told him that I had done it. He really started giving it to me on the bench. And to make it worse, one of the many "chiefs" who had taken over the coaching for this one game came over and started yelling at me too.

"Fleming," this guy yelled at me, "you're nothing but a prima donna, and if you learned to keep your mouth shut sometimes, you'd get along a little better!"

That just ate me up. I had yelled at our player so that he wouldn't get hurt, and I had to take all this noise. So after the game I told them just exactly what they could do with their club, and I packed my bag and went home. I thought to myself that I was young enough; I could just give up hockey and go back to school. The truth was, I didn't know what I was going to do.

The next day I went to see Kenny Reardon. Even though I was pretty sure he never liked me much, he had been the person who originally scouted me, and I thought maybe he could help. Kenny wasn't there, but Frank Selke, Jr., was, and I told him what had happened. I also told him about all the vague promises Pollock had given me and about how I couldn't even understand why I had to play for Kingston. He placated me with a story about how they really needed hockey players and how I was simply going to have to swallow my pride. It was tough, but I did, and eventually I went back to Kingston to finish the season.

Right up until the last two games of the season I only had 14 goals, and I really wanted to finish with 20. So we went to Sudbury, and I ended up scoring the hat trick and a couple of assists. Then we went to Three Rivers and I scored two goals there. Counting that goal with Rochester I had scored 20, so I felt that I had salvaged something out of a bad year.

I found out that I had been scouted by Chicago that season, and in the spring I discovered I was going to be traded to the Black Hawks.

That summer I worked at a golf course with Dickie Moore, and I told him I needed advice on how to make the Black Hawks team at training camp. He gave me some really good advice: "Look at the list and see who the returning veterans are and who the rookies will be. It's the rookies you have to beat, so every time you get a chance to run into them, do it. Knock them on their fannies, beat them to the puck, beat them checking, beat them any way you can, but beat them. And don't let the veterans think they've got it made — hit them, too. Just let everybody know that you're there."

And that's exactly what I did. There were three other fellows I had to worry about when I got to training camp: Ab McDonald, who had played with Montreal and had the ability and experience to make the club; "Cece" Hoekstra, a good skater who wasn't quite aggressive enough; and Bob Courcy, a tremendous hockey player. Courcy had everything — skating ability, puck sense, and a good shot. But Courcy didn't have the heart, as it turned out. So I stuck it out at camp until the last day, holding my breath to see if I would make it. And when the moment came, no one took me aside and gave me the word individually. They just walked into the dressing room on the last day and posted a printed list — and I was in!

When I first sat on a bench in the National League, I still

didn't know if I was a forward or a defenseman. I just sat and filled in wherever Rudy Pilous, our coach, wanted me. I never complained. I just enjoyed it and practiced hard. But I love the game, and when a player just sits on the bench, the adrenalin keeps on flowing. So when I got on the ice, I gave it everything I had, and when friction developed on the ice, I dropped gloves and fought. I didn't take the time to think about the fact that if the opposition retaliates, they'll get the penalty. I just thought about how I have to stay in the league, how I have to fight back so they'll know I won't be pushed around. This has always been my way.

I found out very early in my NHL career that my aggressiveness was my passport. The first time we played in New York, Andy Bathgate and Stan Mikita got into a fight, and Mikita was getting the worst of it. But when Ranger defenseman John Hanna made a move to join the fracas, I grabbed him and told him to let them fight it out. After the fight and the period were over, Pilous took me aside in the dressing room.

"Do you see the color of his jersey?" he said, pointing to Mikita. "Well, the color of your jersey is the same. And if anyone else on your team gets into trouble, you get in there and help if you want to play for this club."

Needless to say, that little bit of advice stuck in my mind when we went out to play the next period. Right away I had to stop Dean Prentice from going out to the point in a face-off, and I got in front of him. He didn't like that at all, so he shoved me. Off came my gloves and I threw a few good punches at him. That was my first fight, but later Eddie Shack and I had a row that was really something.

At one point I checked Shack, and then he checked me, and we started to fight. I still had the stick in my hands as I chased him around the net. New York's goalie, Jack McCartan, threw his stick to Shack, and as he did it, he hit me. Then Shack and I got to center ice, and I was about to spear him, but he buckled over. I hadn't touched him yet, but as he buckled, I dropped my gloves and hit him with a jab in the face, sort of a sucker punch. After we broke up, we skated back to pick up our sticks and gloves, and McCartan was there to pick up his stick. Suddenly it flashed through my mind that McCartan had hit me with his goalie's stick. I didn't bother to think about whether he had done it deliberately or accidentally; I just remembered that he hit me. So I jammed him one in the face. And John Hanna couldn't stand by and watch me pound the goalie, so he went at me. And that was my first big fracas in the NHL — I got a total of 37 penalty minutes in that one game!

During the years previous to that moment, I had never really known whether I would make it. I didn't really have another vocation, and I'm sure that had I never made it to the National League, I would have remained with the game. I love it and everything connected with it.

But now I don't know whether I would consider going back down into the minors if it came to that. Even though I play with Buffalo now, I have committed myself to a home outside Chicago and to a business there during the off season. I guess it would depend on whom I'd play for and how much I'd make. Or I might go back down to coach; I think I'd like that. If I could help another individual to make it up to the NHL, I'd be very content because it's really the only place to play. It's like they say about climbing that ladder; there are a lot of steps getting to the top, but only one step to fall all the way down. The truth is I really don't want to see that last step.

"No one ever said to me, 'You're going up in a couple of years.' "

— *Ernie Wakely*

9

Ernie Wakely

When Ernie Wakely of the St. Louis Blues was named to the West Division All-Star team at mid-season, 1970-1971, it was the culmination of one of the longest journeys through the minors ever experienced by a professional athlete.

Wakely's career as a goalie started in the distant town of Flin Flon, Manitoba, and wended its way south to St. Boniface, Manitoba, and Winnipeg. Manitoba; then east to Ottawa, Ontario, Kingston, Ontario, North Bay, Ontario, and Montreal, Quebec.

Eventually, the thin, 5'11", 160-pound Wakely made it to the United States, and he played in such cities as Spokane, Omaha, Cleveland, Seattle, and Houston. But it was always in the minors: ten years and hundreds of thousands of miles by bus, train, and plane, from the Atlantic coast to the Pacific.

In a sense, it was Wakely's misfortune to develop his hockey skills in the Montreal Canadiens' farm system. During the sixties, when Ernie was waiting for his big chance,

*Montreal had one of the most powerful teams in the NHL,
and the club was especially strong in goal. In fourteen
seasons the Canadiens won the Vezina Trophy nine times.
Wakely's chances for cracking that kind of lineup was not
very good.*

*Still he plugged away, and in July 1969, the big break
developed when St. Louis traded a couple of minor league
forwards to Montreal for Wakely. The St. Louis Blues also
had veterans Glenn Hall and Jacques Plante, both splendid
goaltenders. Even against the competitive background, however, Wakely came through. Plante eventually went to
Toronto, Hall became number two St. Louis goalie, and
Wakely achieved his lifelong objective — playing regularly in
the NHL.*

F LIN Flon, Manitoba, where I learned how to
be a goalkeeper, is an unusual town. It got its name in a
strange way. In 1915, a man discovered deposits of gold,
copper, zinc, and silver at the site where the place eventually
was settled.

It so happened that the man also found a novel called *The
Sunless City* (by J.E. Preston-Muddock) on the ground. He
read the novel and discovered that its hero was Professor
Josiah Flintabbatey Flonatin. The founder subtracted a few
letters here and there and called the town Flin Flon.

Hockey is a very big part of the life of Flin Flon. We have
a Junior team there called the Bombers and lots of hockey
for kids. I got my start at the local arena where all the
hockey programs were held. I was about seven when I first
got involved with the game.

My father was working as a foreman in the local mines at
the time so we weren't badly off, and there was no trouble
getting equipment like skates and sticks. And there was never
any problem finding ice. If we weren't using the arena, we'd
be on the lakes or ponds around Flin Flon.

When I started in organized hockey, I played forward, but that wasn't such a good move because my ability as a forward wasn't top-notch, and I didn't get much ice because there were so many players on the team. The coach wanted to go with the best so that he could win. One day our goaltender didn't show up, and there was no substitute. I said I would take a crack at goalkeeping and the coach said it was all right with him. I never played any other position again.

We went on to win that first game, and the coach liked the way I played. That was the Peewee level of the Flin Flon hockey organization. For me it was fun, but my mother had some reservations about it.

I was the only child in the family and my mother was concerned about my getting hurt — she still is — and she always worried. In a way, she had good reason. At age nine, after only three years of playing hockey, I had lost nine teeth.

The whole accident was ironic. We were getting ready for a championship series, so the league directors called off the regular games temporarily to be sure we didn't get hurt in advance of the championship. Instead, we had an all-star practice, and I played in the nets. For some reason there was a light missing in the arena, making it a little darker than usual.

One of the forwards skated in on me for a shot and put the puck higher than usual. Instead of standing up, I went down and got the puck right in the kisser. That took care of nine teeth with one shot.

That didn't curb my enthusiasm. I always walked around the house telling my mother, "I'm going to play hockey; I'm going to play for the Rangers." For some reason I always wanted to play for New York, although I never had a favorite player as such. We were so far away from the rest of the world that we didn't hear too much about the big league players. I got to like the Rangers because New York sponsored our Junior club at the time.

Each season I improved a little bit more, and by 1958 I was a pretty fair goaltender. It was then I had to decide whether I'd stay in Flin Flon and play my hockey there or go elsewhere since I was 17 and still in school, and I realized that the Flin Flon team would be on the road a lot and that that would keep me away from school. Flin Flon is so remote that the Bombers had to travel a lot.

I couldn't afford to be on the road for two weeks at a time unless I quit school, and I didn't want to do that. Somehow, the Winnipeg Junior team worked out a deal with Flin Flon, enabling me to go south to Winnipeg, and I played my first season with the Braves in 1958-1959 in the Manitoba Junior Hockey League. Moving to Winnipeg was a major change in my life because it is one of Canada's largest cities, whereas Flin Flon is quite small.

I played for the Braves through the 1960-1961 season, and I also got a shot at the Winnipeg Warriors, which was then the city's pro team in the Western League. My first break with the Warriors happened toward the end of the season in 1960. The club wasn't very good and was destined to finish out of the playoffs. The only things I remember about the experience are that the team didn't fare too well and that I was awfully nervous.

Strangely enough, after playing so much as a Junior, I began to play less as a professional. My first full year as a pro was in 1961-1962, for the Hull-Ottawa Canadiens in the Eastern Professional League, which is no longer in existence.

Up until then the farthest east I had ever traveled was to Sudbury, in northern Ontario, when my parents traveled to Elliot Lake for some uranium mining. Well, in that same season in which I had gone east to Ottawa I also played for the North Bay Trappers and the Kingston Frontenacs of the same Eastern Pro League.

In the Eastern League it was possible for one club to

"loan" a player to another club if the second club needed a player. Kingston's goaltender had been hurt, and the club needed a replacement, so that's where I came in. I played three games for Kingston. When I went back to Ottawa, I found out that the North Bay goaltender had had a nervous breakdown, so I went north and played six games in North Bay.

While I was in Ottawa I was playing second-fiddle to Cesare Maniago, the regular goalie, so I really enjoyed being loaned to other teams because I was getting to play; that's what every young goalie wants and needs. But I belonged to the Montreal Canadiens' organization and, at the time, nobody suggested to me that I'd ever have a chance in the National Hockey League.

I know that other players in my shoes had been told by the big league coaches that they would probably be called up soon. But no one ever said to me, "You're going up in a couple of years."

It seemed everybody was getting a chance. I got mine in the 1962-1963 season, the same year I won the goalie award in the Eastern League. Jacques Plante, the regular Canadiens goalie at the time, got sick. Maniago was the one who was supposed to take Plante's place, but he was all the way out in Spokane, and he couldn't get back in time.

I was in Ottawa at the time, and Sammy Pollock, who ran our team, drove me to Montreal for the game. We didn't talk much because I didn't want to. If I talked too much about the game, I'd get too nervous.

That night I went up against the Rangers, the team I had wanted to play for when I was a kid. In the dressing room I sat oppostite some of the greats of hockey — Jean Beliveau, Henri Richard, and Bernie Geoffrion.

I was really nervous. I had never played in front of a crowd that large; something like 14,000 people were in the Forum.

In the dressing room I sat next to Geoffrion, and he tried to help. "Relax," said Geoffrion, "it's just like any other game. We'll be working for you."

But New York scored first and looked good. Then, just as Geoffrion had said, the Canadiens started working for me and scored six goals. We won the game, 6-3, and I felt pretty good. Meanwhile, the Canadiens had gotten Maniago from Spokane, so when it was all over, I went on the road trip with the Canadiens as the stand-in for Maniago. Then I returned to Ottawa with one NHL game under my belt.

If I had any illusions about going back to the NHL in a hurry, they were dispelled in time. After that game in the Forum, I played in Spokane that season and for Omaha and Quebec the following season. At Quebec I had the most shutouts (3) and the best goals against average (1.90).

The Canadiens didn't call me, though, and in the 1964-1965 season I played in Cleveland, Quebec, and Omaha. The following season I was split between Cleveland, Quebec, and Seattle. Naturally, I became discouraged, and I began to wonder just how much longer it would keep going on like that. To encourage myself I kept telling myself that I should play just one more year.

I had some periods of self-doubt. I would think to myself, "If I'm as good as I think I am, if I have so much ability, then how come I'm not in the major leagues?"

Some people may think it was a lot of fun traveling all over the continent, but for me the constant moving became awfully tiresome. We'd play three or four games in four nights, and it really started to get to me. We'd play one game in one town one night and then have another game someplace else the next night. So we'd travel all night after the game. We didn't usually go by plane or train. We'd bus it from one city to another. So by the time we'd get to our next city, it was pretty late and we were pretty tired. And then we'd have to play another game.

Switching from team to team was uncomfortable because I was always leaving my family, and I never knew how long I'd be in any one city. It might start off being two or three days and wind up being a month away from my family.

Meanwhile, the Canadiens were going through a lot of goalies — Plante, Maniago, Charlie Hodge, Gump Worsley — and it seemed that every year there was somebody new. Every year it would be a new face and he'd do great.

In the 1966-1967 season I played the entire season for Cleveland. I gave up 216 goals in 70 games for 3.09 goals against average, and I looked forward to the NHL expansion. Unfortunately, I wasn't picked by any of the teams, and I was very dejected. I had waited so long, and it looked as if no one wanted me. It was really the low point in my career. But once again I said to myself "Ernie, just one more year, just one more try. See what happens and then decide whether you want to stay in this game."

I played for the Houston Apollos in the Central Pro League for the 1967-1968 season. The weather was warm and nice down there, but the rink made life tough for a hockey player. We couldn't get practice ice at the home rink, and the arena itself was pretty bad.

The big problem with the Houston rink was the lighting, and that can be murder on a goalie. Lighting was so poor there that the goalies could hardly even see the puck when it was shot. It was almost pitch black in the place because they only had ten lights covering the ice itself. I was always thankful when I got out of there without getting hit in the face with the puck. That was before I started wearing a face mask.

Meanwhile, the question kept nagging me — when am I going to make it? And I began to realize that I didn't want to spend all my life down in the minors. "Maybe it's time to get out of the business and get a regular job and settle down," I told myself.

The 1968-1969 season came along and my contract was all right, so I came back for another year on the assumption that it would be a year-to-year thing for me. My problem was that I had no other employment to turn to if I quit hockey. Until I got something that I could really do I had to stay with hockey. I kept thinking I could make it in the NHL, but there really was no way of knowing unless I got the chance.

I finally enrolled in a computer programming course and was studying for that during the summer of 1969. This was supposed to give me something to fall back on if I decided to quit pro hockey. This was in Albuquerque, New Mexico, where I had been living in the off-season, because my parents had moved there from Elliot Lake, and my father got a job there at a uranium mine.

In July 1969, when I was attending the computer programming course, my wife called me. My first reaction was that she was sick and wanted me to go home. But she said we had just received a telegram from Scotty Bowman, the St. Louis Blues' manager, and that I had been traded to St. Louis by Montreal for Norm Beaudin and Bobby Schmautz. When I heard that I nearly fell off my chair. I knew that this was my big chance. At the time, the Blues had Jacques Plante, who was 40, and Glenn Hall, 39, in goal, and I knew they couldn't go on forever. Anyway, I knew that I could get to watch those guys up close and learn a lot of things from them.

So I joined the Blues for the 1969-70 season as the third goaltender, behind Hall and Plante. Oddly enough, the first game I played for St. Louis was against my old favorite team, the Rangers, in New York. I had been injured in training camp and was out for about a month. The finger on my catching hand had been broken, and by the time it had healed, the season was well underway, and I wasn't in tip-top condition. But this was the NHL. I knew I had to come around and perform.

I started working out with the club, and I got a lot of help from Jacques and Glenn. I didn't even have to ask them. They'd often come over and offer the help. But learning was more than that; it was also the opportunity to watch them in action, to pick up things and to be watched by them and told what I was doing wrong.

My first game wasn't good for me in the scoring sense because the Rangers put about six goals past me. Then we went to Boston and tied. But eventually we returned to St. Louis, and I won the game. I played 30 games over the season and allowed only 58 goals for a 2.11 goals against average, best for any goalie playing part-time.

I guess one of the highlights was my first NHL shutout. That was really something. Hall had decided to retire at the start of the season; that meant that Jacques and I were the two goaltenders. But then Glenn decided to return, and the St. Louis fans were all excited about that. My confidence was just beginning to settle in after a few games and I was feeling pretty good. But Hall had returned to St. Louis, and I went into the nets the night he arrived at the St. Louis Arena. The fans were really up for that.

We were up aginst Pittsburgh that night. Hall and Plante came out on the ice at the start of the game to receive the Vezina Trophy as the best goaltenders. I felt tense and pressured. I wanted to do well in front of them, and I did. I came up with my first NHL shutout.

As things turned out, the three goalie system worked. I got in 30 games, we finished first, and I played 3-2/3 games in the playoffs. I began to feel more and more secure; I felt that I could unpack my suitcase and stay awhile. But I never became overconfident. I played each season at a time, trying to learn as much as possible while I could. Jacques was a terrific teacher. He always helped me if I was doing something wrong. I listened to him because I'm always grateful for advice. If I couldn't take advice from a top star like Jacques, I wouldn't be much of a player.

After that season Plante was traded to Toronto, and I was

sorry to see him go. On the other hand, I knew that his leaving would give me a chance to play more games for St. Louis. That was the case in 1970-1971, and I began to think of possibly getting ten years in the NHL. Then I reminded myself to take every year as it comes.

In a sense I was lucky. It was a long, hard drive, but I wound up in St. Louis, a great hockey city, and that made the grind worthwhile. One thing is for sure — I haven't forgotten my ten years in the minors. It's hard to block that much time out of a person's mind. When a player gets to the major leagues, he doesn't automatically forget everything that went before it. He remembers.

He has to.

Records and Vital Statistics

These abbreviations are used in the charts on the following pages:

A	Assists	NHL	National Hockey League
AHL	American Hockey League	OHA	Ontario Hockey Association
AVG	Average	PM	Penalty minutes
CPHL	Central Pacific Hockey League	QHL	Quebec Hockey League
EHL	Eastern Hockey League	SJHL	Quebec Junior Hockey League
G	Goals	SJHL	Saskatchewan Jr. Hockey League
GA	Goals against	SO	Shutouts
GP	Games played	TP	Total points
IHL	International Hockey League	WHL	Western Hockey League
MJHL	Manitoba Junior Hockey League		

* For goalies, asterisk signifies either lowest average in league or most shutouts for season in league. For all other players, asterisk signifies season high in penalty minutes for scoring.

Leslie John (Les) Binkley

GOALTENDER (shoots right). 6' 170 pounds
Born: June 6, 1934. Owen Sound, Ontario

Binkley was trainer of Cleveland Barons during 1957-1958 season and did not play. Won Dudley "Red" Garrett Memorial Trophy in 1961-1962. Missed 1964 playoffs with head injury. Won Harry Holmes Memorial Trophy in 1965-1966 season. Missed start of 1969-1970 season with pulled stomach muscle and part of season with leg injury.

Year	Team	League	GP	GA	SO	AVG
1951-1952	Galt Black Hawks	Jr. "A" OHA	47	180	*4	3.83
1952-1953	Galt Balck Hawks	Jr. "A" OHA	55	213	1	3.87
1953-1954	Galt-Kitchener	Jr. "A" OHA	58	267	0	4.60
1954-1955	Walkerton	Sr. "B" OHA	—	—	—	—
1954-1955	Kitchener Dutchmen	Sr. "A" OHA	3	12	0	4.00
1955-1956	Fort Wayne Komets	IHL	3	13	0	4.33
1955-1956	Baltimore Clippers	EHL	59	302	0	5.11
1956-1957	Charlotte Clippers	EHL	64	239	0	3.73
1957-1958	Did not play.					
1958-1959	Toledo Mercurys	IHL	52	205	1	3.94
1958-1959	Cleveland Barons	AHL	1	3	0	3.00
1959-1960	Toledo Mercurys	IHL	67	294	2	4.39
1960-1961	Toledo Mercurys	IHL	1	0	1	0.00
1960-1961	Cleveland Barons	AHL	8	11	0	1.38
1961-1962	Cleveland Barons	AHL	60	181	5	3.02
1962-1963	Cleveland Barons	AHL	63	203	4	3.22
1963-1964	Cleveland Barons	AHL	65	180	3	2.77
1964-1965	Cleveland Barons (1)	AHL	40	152	0	3.91
1965-1966	Cleveland Barons	AHL	66	192	2	*2.93
1966-1967	San Diego Gulls	WHL	53⅓	190	1	3.56
1967-1968	Pittsburgh Penguins	NHL	54	151	6	2.88
1968-1969	Pittsburgh Penguins	NHL	50	158	0	3.29
1969-1970	Pittsburgh Penguins	NHL	27	79	3	3.21
1970-1971	Pittsburgh Penguins	NHL	34	89	2	2.85
	NHL totals		165	477	11	2.89

(1) — Received one assist.

Dennis William Hull

LEFT WING (shoots left). 6' 185 pounds
Born: November 19, 1944. Pointe Anne, Ontario

Year	Team	League	GP	G	A	TP	PM
1960-1961	St. Cath. Teepees	Jr. "A"					
		OHA	47	6	4	10	—
1961-1962	St. Cath. Teepees	Jr. "A"					
		OHA	50	6	12	18	—
1962-1963	St. Cath. Black Hawks	Jr. "A"					
		OHA	50	19	29	48	—
1963-1964	St. Cath. B. Hawks (1)	Jr. "A"					
		OHA	55	48	49	97	—
1964-1965	Chicago Black Hawks	NHL	55	10	4	14	18
1965-1966	Chicago Black Hawks	NHL	25	1	5	6	6
1965-1966	St. Louis Braves	CPHL	40	11	16	27	14
1966-1967	Chicago Black Hawks	NHL	70	25	17	42	33
1967-1968	Chicago Black Hawks	NHL	74	18	15	33	34
1968-1969	Chicago Black Hawks	NHL	72	30	34	64	25
1969-1970	Chicago Black Hawks	NHL	76	17	35	52	31
1970-1971	Chicago Black Hawks	NHL	78	40	26	66	16
	NHL totals		**450**	**141**	**136**	**277**	**163**

(1) — Member of first all-star team.

Edward Charles (Ed) Van Impe

DEFENSEMAN (shoots left). 5'10" 185 pounds
Born: May 27, 1940. Saskatoon, Saskatchewan.

Van Impe suffered fractured left cheekbone during 1967-1968 season and wore protective mask. Captain of Philadelphia Flyers since 1968-1969.

Year	Team	League	GP	G	A	TP	PM
1957-1958	Saskatoon Jr. Quakers	SJHL	49	2	2	2	58
1958-1959	Saskatoon Jr. Quakers	SJHL	48	0	23	23	*150
1959-1960	Saskatoon Quakers (1)	SJHL	—	—	—	—	136
1960-1961	Calgary Stampeders	WHL	66	4	15	19	123
1961-1962	Buffalo Bisons (2)	AHL	70	0	19	19	172
1962-1963	Buffalo Bisons	AHL	65	3	12	15	*196
1963-1964	Buffalo Bisons	AHL	70	4	22	26	*193
1964-1965	Buffalo Bisons	AHL	72	5	6	11	197
1965-1966	Buffalo Bisons	AHL	70	9	28	37	153
1966-1967	Chicago Black Hawks (3)	NHL	61	8	11	19	111
1967-1968	Philadelphia Flyers	NHL	67	4	13	17	141
1968-1969	Philadelphia Flyers	NHL	68	7	12	19	112
1969-1970	Philadelphia Flyers	NHL	65	0	10	10	117
1970-1971	Philadelphia Flyers	NHL	77	0	11	11	80
NHL totals			338	19	57	76	561

(1) — Member of second all-star team.

(2) — Led in penalties during play offs with 25 minutes.

(3) — Drafted from Chicago by Philadelphia Flyers in NHL Expansion Draft, June, 1967.

Jean Ratelle

CENTER (shoots left). 6'1" 175 pounds
Born: October 3, 1940. Lac St. Jean, Quebec

Missed start of 1966-1967 season due to surgery for slipped disc.

Year	Team	League	GP	G	A	TP	PM
1958-1959	Guelph Biltmores	Jr. "A"					
		OHA	54	20	31	51	—
1959-1960	Guelph Biltmores	Jr. "A"					
		OHA	48	39	47	86	—
1959-1960	Three Rivers Lions	EPHL	3	3	5	8	0
1960-1961	Guelph Royals (1)	Jr. "A"					
		OHA	47	40	*61	101	—
1960-1961	New York Rangers	NHL	3	2	1	3	0
1961-1962	New York Rangers	NHL	31	4	8	12	4
1961-1962	Kitchener-Waterloo						
	Beavers	EPHL	32	10	29	39	8
1962-1963	New York Rangers	NHL	48	11	9	20	8
1962-1963	Baltimore Clippers	AHL	20	11	8	19	0
1963-1964	Baltimore Clippers	AHL	57	20	26	46	2
1963-1964	New York Rangers	NHL	15	0	7	7	6
1964-1965	Baltimore Clippers	AHL	8	9	4	13	6
1964-1965	New York Rangers	NHL	54	14	21	35	14
1965-1966	New York Rangers	NHL	67	21	30	51	10
1966-1967	New York Rangers	NHL	41	6	5	11	4
1967-1968	New York Rangers	NHL	74	32	46	78	18
1968-1969	New York Rangers	NHL	75	32	46	78	26
1969-1970	New York Rangers	NHL	75	32	42	74	28
1970-1971	New York Rangers	NHL	78	26	46	72	14
	NHL totals		**561**	**180**	**261**	**441**	**132**

(1) — Member of second all-star team.

John Bowie Ferguson

RIGHT WING (shoots left). 6' 190 pounds
Born: September 5, 1938. Vancouver, British Columbia

Ferguson was captain of Melville Millionaires in 1958-1959. Was non-playing coach of Montreal team in new professional lacrosse league in 1968. Missed part of 1967-1968 season with broken right hand. Set record for penalty minutes in 1968-1969 Stanley Cup Playoffs (80) and is all-time leader in penalty minutes during playoffs. Fractured thumb in pre-season exhibition game and missed start of 1969-1970 season. Refractured right thumb and suffered fractured right cheekbone requiring surgery during the 1969-1970 season. Retired beginning of 1970-1971 season, but returned to Canadiens November 17, 1970.

Year	Team	League	GP	G	A	TP	PM
1957-1958	Melville Millionaires	SJHL	50	14	30	43½	100
1958-1959	Melville Millionaires	SJHL	44	32	34	66	83
1959-1960	Fort Wayne Komets	IHL	68	32	33	65	126
1960-1961	Cleveland Barons	AHL	62	13	21	34	126
1961-1962	Cleveland Barons	AHL	70	20	21	41	146
1962-1963	Cleveland Barons (1)	AHL	72	38	40	78	179
1963-1964	Montreal Canadiens	NHL	59	18	27	45	125
1964-1965	Montreal Canadiens	NHL	69	17	27	44	156
1965-1966	Montreal Canadiens (2)	NHL	65	11	14	25	153
1966-1967	Montreal Canadiens	NHL	67	20	22	42	*177
1967-1968	Montreal Canadiens	NHL	61	15	18	33	117
1968-1969	Montreal Canadiens (3)	NHL	71	29	23	52	185
1969-1970	Montreal Canadiens (4)	NHL	48	19	13	32	139
1970-1971	Montreal Canadiens	NHL	60	16	14	30	162
	NHL totals		**500**	**145**	**158**	**303**	**1214**

(1) — Member of first all-star team.
(2) — Led in penalties, during the play off with 44 minutes.
(3) — Led in penalties during play off with 80 minutes.
(4) — Drew six game suspension from NHL, November 1969

Norman Douglas (Doug) Barkley

FORMER DEFENSEMAN (shoots right). 6'2" 195 pounds. Born: January 6, 1937. Lethbridge, Alberta

Starting fourth season with Detroit, Barkley was best scorer of team's rearguards in his next-to-last season with 5-20-25. Topped league's defensemen in goals during 1963-1964 with 11. Lost Calder Trophy in rookie year by two-tenths of point to Toronto's Kent Douglas. WHL record holder for most goals by defenseman, with 25 in 1961-1962. Worked in Detroit Red Wing organization as administrative assistant 1966-1969. Became coach of Detroit's minor league farm team, Fort Worth Wings, 1969. Called up to coach NHL Detroit Red Wings during first half of 1970-1971 season.

Year	Team	League	GP	G	A	TP	PM
1956-1957	Calgary Stampeders	WHL	63	4	8	12	112
1957-1958	Calgary Stampeders	WHL	31	3	5	8	72
1957-1958	Chicago Black Hawks	NHL	3	0	0	0	0
1957-1958	Buffalo Bisons	AHL	27	0	3	3	22
1958-1959	Buffalo Bisons	AHL	55	2	5	7	59
1959-1960	Calgary Stampeders	WHL	55	7	18	25	82
1959-1960	Chicago Black Hawks	NHL	3	0	0	0	2
1960-1961	Buffalo Bisons	AHL	66	9	28	37	106
1961-1962	Calgary Stampeders	WHL	70	25	49	74	82
1962-1963	Detroit Red Wings	NHL	70	3	24	27	78
1963-1964	Detroit Red Wings	NHL	67	11	21	32	115
1964-1965	Detroit Red Wings	NHL	67	5	20	25	122
1965-1966	Detroit Red Wings	NHL	43	5	15	20	65
	NHL totals		253	24	80	104	382

Reginald Stephen (Reggie) Fleming

LEFT WING (shoots left). 5'10" 185 pounds
Born: April 21, 1936. Montreal, Quebec.

Fleming set NHL record with 37 penalty minutes in single game, October 19, 1960. Record broken by Jim Dorey (1968-1969).

Year	Team	League	GP	G	A	TP	PM
1954-1955	Montreal Jr. Canadiens	QJHL	44	3	11	14	*139
1955-1956	Toronto St. Michaels	Jr. "A"					
		OHA	42	1	8	9	—
1956-1957	Shawinigan Falls Cataracts	QHL	61	2	9	11	109
1957-1958	Shawinigan Falls Cataracts	QHL	51	6	15	21	*227
1958-1959	Rochester Americans	AHL	70	6	16	22	112
1959-1960	Kingston Frontenacs	EPHL	52	19	49	68	91
1959-1960	Rochester Americans	AHL	9	1	5	6	4
1959-1960	Montreal Canadiens (1)	NHL	3	0	0	0	2
1960-1961	Chicago Black Hawks	NHL	66	4	4	8	145
1961-1962	Chicago Black Hawks	NHL	70	7	9	16	71
1962-1963	Chicago Black Hawks	NHL	64	7	7	14	99
1963-1964	Chicago Black Hawks (2)	NHL	61	3	6	9	140
1964-1965	Boston Bruins	NHL	67	18	23	41	136
1965-1966	Boston Bruins (3)	NHL	34	4	6	10	42
1965-1966	New York Rangers (4)	NHL	35	10	14	24	124
1966-1967	New York Rangers	NHL	61	15	16	31	146
1967-1968	New York Rangers	NHL	73	17	7	24	132
1968-1969	New York Rangers (5)	NHL	72	8	12	20	138
1969-1970	Philadelphia Flyers (6)	NHL	65	9	18	27	134
1970-1971	Buffalo Sabres	NHL	78	6	10	16	159
NHL totals			**749**	**108**	**132**	**240**	**1468**

(1) — Traded to Chicago Black Hawks by Montreal Canadiens with Bob Courcy, Ab McDonald and Cecil Hoesktra for Glen Skov, 3 other players and cash, June, 1960.

(2) — Traded to Boston by Chicago with Ab McDonald for Doug Mohns, June, 1964.

(3) — Traded to New York Rangers by Boston for John McKenzie, January, 1966.

(4) — Led NHL in penalties with combined total (Boston-New York) of 166 minutes.

(5) — Traded to Philadelphia Flyers by New York Rangers for Leon Rochefort, June, 1969. (N.Y. also purchased Don Blackburn from Philadelphia following 1969 NHL Draft as part of the deal).

(6) — Drafted from Philadelphia Flyers by Buffalo Sabres, June, 1970.

Ernest Alfred (Ernie) Wakely

GOALTENDER (shoots left). 5'11" 160 pounds
Born: November 27, 1940. Flin Flon, Manitoba

Wakely started wearing mask in January, 1969. Set CHL playoff record
with 3 shutouts in 1964.

Year	Team	League	GP	GA	SO	AVG
1958-1959	Winnipeg Braves	MJHL	—	—	—	3.56
1959-1960	Winnipeg Braves	MJHL	—	—	—	—
1959-1960	Winnipeg Warriors	WHL	4	16	0	4.00
1960-1961	Winnipeg Braves	MJHL	—	—	—	—
1960-1961	Winnipeg Warriors	WHL	9	43	0	4.77
1961-1962	Hull-Ottawa Canadiens	EPHL	2	4	0	2.00
1961-1962	Kingston Frontenacs	EPHL	3	10	0	3.33
1961-1962	North Bay Trappers	EPHL	6	18	0	3.00
1962-1963	Montreal Canadiens	NHL	1	3	0	3.00
1962-1963	Spokane Comets	WHL	3	16	0	5.33
1962-1963	Hull-Ottawa Canadiens (1)	EPHL	41	122	*2	*2.97
1963-1964	Omaha Knights	CPHL	59	173	2	*2.93
1963-1964	Quebec Aces (2)	AHL	8	33	0	4.12
1964-1965	Omaha Knights	CPHL	15	40	0	2.67
1964-1965	Cleveland-Quebec	AHL	30	126	1	4.13
1965-1966	Cleveland-Quebec	AHL	1-1/3	7	0	5.25
1965-1966	Seattle Totems	WHL	26-2/3	88	2	3.30
1966-1967	Cleveland Barons	AHL	70	216	0	3.09
1967-1968	Houston Apollos (3)	CPHL	57	163	1	2.95
1968-1969	Cleveland Barons (3)	AHL	65	210	1	3.27
1968-1969	Montreal Canadiens (4)	NHL	1	4	0	4.00
1969-1970	St. Louis Blues	NHL	30	58	4	*2.11
1970-1971	St. Louis Blues	NHL	51	133	3	2.79
	NHL totals (4)		**83**	**198**	**7**	**2.39**

(1) — Won EPHL Leading Goalie Award.
(2) — Leading goalie in play off (1.90) and had most shutouts (3).
(3) — Member of second all-star team.
(4) — Traded to St. Louis Blues by Montreal Canadiens for Norm Beaudin
     and Bobby Schmautz, July, 1969.